An Adventure Into The Tarot

Next to the Ouija Board, no "tool" has generated more controversy than Tarot cards. Can what the author calls a "party ice-breaker" devastate lives and destroy self-esteem? Or is the Tarot deck like Jacob's ladder, leading to Heaven?

In this original examination of the Biblical prohibition against divination—and just what Tarot cards and readers can and can't do—noted scholar, author and lecturer Jacqueline Lichtenberg approaches these questions from Biblical, sociological, psychological and scientific viewpoints.

Natural Law, fortune telling, God's will, predestiny, devil worship, extrasensory perception, the Qabalah and free will are some of the thought-provoking areas covered in this groundbreaking book, the first in a series.

No matter how you view Tarot cards, there is incontrovertible evidence that Tarot cards are doorways. By the time you finish reading this book, you will be able to answer the question: Will you step through?

Books in this series

Volume One

Never Cross A Palm With Silver

by Jacqueline Lichtenberg

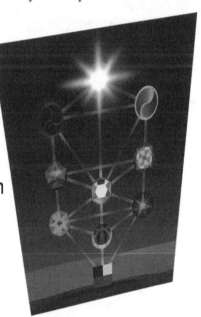

A radical new
approach to the
Bible, divination
and destiny.

Belfry
Books

The Biblical Tarot
Volume 1, Never Cross A Palm With Silver

Published by

 Belfry Books

Toad Hall, Inc.
Rural Route 2 Box 16-B
Laceyville, PA 18623

(717) 869-2942
FAX (717) 869-1031

Dedication

To Gene Roddenberry
May He Rest in Peace

Acknowledgments

Tarot belongs to an area of endeavor which cannot be taught as science is taught but can only be learned. So I must first acknowledge, in no particular order, three people with whom I've learned much, with whom I've conducted the seminars from which the material in the book is drawn, and whose advent in my life demonstrates the need for a spiritual model of reality beyond the scientific.

Katie Filipowicz wrote me my first fan letter for my first published original novel. We later met for the first time at a Star Trek convention where I read her name tag and promptly enlisted her aid during an autographing session. She inevitably was drawn into our group's exploration of the spiritual dimensions of reality.

Anne Pinzow was terrified of the Devil card when she first walked into my house and saw a Tarot layout on the kitchen table. Within a few years, she became much sought after as a Tarot reader, respected all over the East Coast. Using that reputation, she, together with Roberta Klein-Mendelson, another reputable Tarot reader, founded a gathering called Esotericon and drew all of us into the project.

Roberta got the idea for Esotericon from reading Marion Zimmer Bradley's *Mists of Avalon*. Marion had years before given me my first introduction to astrology and related occult disciplines to establish a mutual language in which she could explain to me what was lacking in my fiction.

To date, Esotericon has spun off three other esoteric gatherings: Ecumenicon, Ethericon, and Sacred Space.

At about the time Marion introduced me to astrology, Judy Thomasses introduced me to Tarot, which I soon discovered Marion also knew. At that time, Judy was a beginner, but now she's a well established and respected practitioner and teacher of astrology and Tarot.

There is an invisible thread that ties all these people together: *Star Trek*.

I got Judy involved in the Trek conventions because she loved the show. I read Tarot in public for the first time at a Trek convention. I met Anne at a talk I gave at a library on the Bantam paperback *Star Trek Lives!* which I co-authored. I met my sometime collaborator Jean Lorrah through two friends I first knew via Trek fandom. Jean was already well versed in Tarot, astrology, and palmistry, which helped us collaborate. The same two Trek friends introduced me to Marion. And Roberta came to me through my activities in the fandom surrounding Marion's Darkover novels.

So this book comes to you ultimately because of Gene Roddenberry (1931-1991), creator of *Star Trek* and one of the greatest men of our century. Though his primary orientation was scientific, and he displayed little interest in the occult, his fictional emphasis was on the growth of human wisdom. That, ultimately, is what Tarot is about.

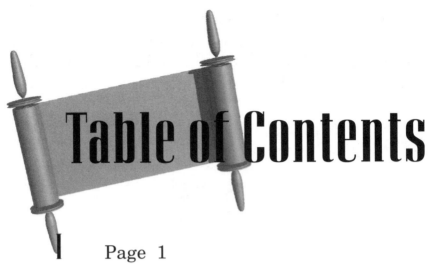

Table of Contents

Why Does The Bible Forbid Divination?

Precisely what activity does the Bible prohibit under the concept "divination"? And, since Tarot is not mentioned by name, does that prohibition really apply to Tarot? Why should someone looking for a Tarot reading care what the Bible says? How can a harmless little card game, a party ice-breaker, devastate lives and destroy self-esteem? Can a fortuneteller actually foresee our future? What is predestiny, exactly? Everybody's heard of black magick, but how many people can really define it? What is it about black magick that makes it "wrong?" And why is it wrong? What does divination really mean?

Why Do Some People Equate Tarot Reading With Devil Worship?

Would an adventure into the Tarot be for you an exposure to the Devil and all his temptations? How do you tell? What is Devil Worship? And why is it wrong? How could the Tarot lead someone into idolatry? What aspect of human nature allows us to avoid emotional and physical pain? Is the Tarot a tool for circumventing the need for God?

III   Page 37

What Are The Real and Present Dangers of Using and/or Learning Tarot?

What does it mean to "read" Tarot? What does a Tarot reader actually do? Why is it important for the symbols hidden within the artistic pictures to be "correct"? What will the Tarot reader do with those symbols that makes the correctness matter? How do you tell whether you want a particular person to read Tarot for you?

IV   Page 52

Why Do Some Tarot Readers Refuse To Accept Money Or Any Material Recompense For Their Readings?

Would a Tarot reader be more prone to make mistakes when getting paid for the work? If you find a Tarot reader who's right for you in your current predicament, how do you decide what would be an appropriate fee? How do you decide if the reader is charging too much, and is therefore likely to be a charlatan who's just pretending to read Tarot?

V   Page 65

Does Learning To Read Tarot Make A Person Become Psychic?

Or can only psychics learn to read Tarot? Or is it that psychic talent has nothing whatever to do with it? What is psychic talent? What is ESP? Where does it come from? What is it good for? Does it even exist? Why can't science prove whether ESP exists or not? Do you need to know the philosophy behind the Tarot?

VI Page 76
Do The Principles Behind Tarot Defy Science?

What is the origin of the Tarot? Did the Tarot come from India? The physical origin of the Tarot may never become known. Does that matter? What has Qabalah to do with the Tarot? Can we find something in the Qabalistic Tree of Life glyph that admits to the reality of the soul and spirit and their efficaciousness in determining the success or failure of any real world endeavor? How does the Tarot work? Does this Tree of Life glyph represent the relationship between God and Man? Why can't science prove God exists?

VII Page 103
How Do You Discern Whether A Tarot Reader Is Skilled Enough And Wise Enough To Help You? What Does a Tarot Reading Really Tell You?

How do you recognize psychological counseling as opposed to the Tarot reading itself? Once you've learned to distinguish Tarot reading from counseling, what do you listen for in a Tarot reader's words to discover whether they're any good at reading Tarot? What can a diviner who is not trying to tell your fortune say? If a Tarot reader tells you that you are under psychic attack, or under some kind of curse, how can you decide if he's bonkers? A charlatan? Or for real?

VIII Page 127
What Can You Do To Get A "Good" Tarot Reading?

Guidelines for Tarot readings. Readings depend solely on the skills and wisdom of the Tarot reader. How to attain and maintain an appropriate level of consciousness—a light trance. What the

Tarot can and can't tell you. How to invoke wardings. How to create a receptive state—the less of the work the Tarot reader has to do and the more the reader will exceed his/her own abilities.

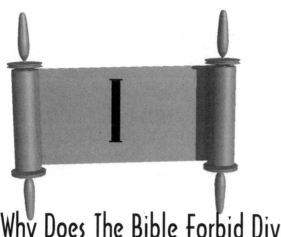

Why Does The Bible Forbid Divination?

People readily agree that Tarot cards can be used for divination, but what is divination—exactly?

People often seek Tarot readings without knowing their own personal definitions of Tarot or divination, and without seriously considering the Biblical prohibition of divination.

People have come to me asking for a Tarot reading when they have never before seen a Tarot deck, except perhaps in boxes at a book store, and have no idea how many cards there are in a Tarot deck, or why there are that number and no other. Seekers have presented themselves as guinea pigs willing to allow a total stranger to experiment on them using the Tarot deck, without having the least idea of what sorts of things a Tarot deck can do—and can't do. When hiring any other consultant, most people consider it worthwhile to become much better informed than that.

For example, they'd know that a surgeon cuts and sews flesh, a dentist drills teeth, an electrician handles dangerous power cables that could burn down your house, and a building contractor can alter a structure and still keep it from falling down on you.

Each of these hired experts is dealing with an aspect of your life that is potentially as deadly dangerous as that dealt with by a Tarot reader. But how many people even know what aspect of themselves they are submitting to a Tarot reading or the Tarot reader's skills?

Can a fortuneteller actually foresee our future?

In the course of growing up in middle-class America, one generally gathers a working knowledge of medicine, electricity, and construction, just enough to know whether to buy an over-the-counter remedy or to go to the doctor. We learn just enough to know that you don't need an electrician to plug in a new appliance, but you do need one to make a new plug. We learn just enough about these things to judge whether the hired expert knows his/her job.

Let's say you know nothing about the Tarot. You might assume that since your parents never taught you how to choose a Tarot

While getting your eybrows waxed, your nails buffed, and your wrinkles removed, how much psychic talent does it take to inform you that you are preparing for a "special event"?

reader, then it can't be nearly as tricky or as critical as picking a doctor.

As a result, many people have gotten into very bad, very serious, shattering psychological difficulties by tangling with the Tarot. Often, the only way they can recover their self-esteem and rebuild their lives is by turning to a religion that considers the Tarot a tool of the Devil, an evil to be shunned at all costs.

And very often, they do successfully rebuild their lives. The religion then points to these people as proof that the Tarot is evil, that the Tarot itself caused this person to be lured into the Darkness.

On the face of it, the evidence is incontrovertible. There are literally thousands of people who've undergone psychological debilitation as a direct result of encounters with the Tarot. No reasonable person could ignore this evidence that the Tarot is a tool of ultimate evil.

And the penultimate argument in support of the evil inherent in the Tarot is the oft quoted prohibition in the Bible against divination.

This immediately raises two questions: Precisely what activity does the Bible prohibit under the concept "divination"? And, since Tarot is not mentioned by name, does that prohibition really apply to Tarot?

Was the violation of the Biblical injunction the source of the psychological difficulty these people experienced, or could their problems have been caused by some other factor in their behavior?

To discover the exact nature of the prohibited activity loosely translated (via several intermediate, sometimes dead, languages) as divination, one has to go back to the original Hebrew— which itself was a dead language for thousands of years.

Groping into the vastness of this obscure field of linguistics, one can come up with a very simple answer. The Biblical prohibition was aimed at the beggars and charlatans who would sit within the gates of a city and offer—for money—to read futures and fortunes in the clouds, or in rolled knucklebones, or whatever.

In other words, the prohibition was against fortunetellers. It never had anything to do with cards or the Tarot. It had to do with extorting money on the pretext of foreseeing the future for a particular individual.

Most people assume—from the packaging of Tarot decks in book stores—that they are fortune telling cards, and that that's all they are and all they can be used for. Since fortune telling is prohibited, then Tarot cards are prohibited. That's obvious enough.

But having accepted the obvious, most people fail to ask the next obvious question. Why should there be a Biblical injunction against fortune telling? It's fun. It's harmless. And sometimes it's even useful because it gets you thinking about things differently.

Think about it. What's evil about fortune telling? How can a harmless little card game, a party ice-breaker, devastate lives and destroy self-esteem? Nobody really believes the silly things fortunetellers say. So how can it be unhealthy?

One answer comes from archeology and anthropology. In Biblical times, people did really believe that it was possible for a seer to look at passing clouds (or stars or knucklebones or rhinestones or whatever) and know *exactly* what will happen to a particular person.

Today, we tell ourselves we don't really believe that. But what is belief? Who can define it exactly? And does it matter whether we believe it or not? Does not believing it limit the destruction a fortuneteller can sow into our lives?

Consider how we decide whether something is true or not, how we come to believe or disbelieve what is told to us. An idea seems plausible if it fits neatly into our overall view of the universe—our philosophy of life. And it seems ridiculous, a mere superstition for the ignorant primitives, if it doesn't fit into our view of the universe.

Can a fortuneteller actually foresee our future?

If you think so, then you are subscribing to the philosophical stance called Predestination. If you don't think so, you are accepting the philosophy called Free Will.

If you don't have a firm, adamant, and unmoveable stance on the question of whether a fortuneteller can see the future, then this vital cornerstone of your internal epistemology is weak and riddled with confusion. This could leave you open to suggestion or prey to your own neurotic needs.[1]

Here we're getting close to seeing exactly why the Bible would prohibit fortune telling.

1. This is oversimplified. The Predestination/Free Will argument actually has many shades of gray.

The documents forming the Bible share a coherent philosophy which becomes apparent when you compare statements from different contexts.

God created man in His Own image. Image is a tricky word, a slippery word to translate and define. Connotations get lost or politically distorted. What did the original Hebrew really mean? Here's one answer you might find. Image refers more to psychological form than it does to physical form. The Biblical concept of God is a non-material, non-physical, non-engendered concept—a Pillar of Smoke, a Pillar of Fire, a Burning Bush, a Voice.[2] God accomplishes things in the world by Willing them to be, and Saying Words to that effect.

God has given man dominion over the fishes of the sea, etc. When the Bible describes God creating something, the Hebrew word for create actually means to create something out of nothing. That word is never used with reference to what humans create. Instead, a different word is used which means to create something out of something. (Even *Star Trek's* transporter and synthesizers create matter out of energy, and energy is something, not nothing.)

And so it is argued that part of the "image" of God repeated in humanity is this dominion that God has given to humanity, the ability to perform the same kind of function that God per-

2. There are, of course, also references to the "outstretched hand" and the "right arm" and to sitting on a throne. Don't ever stop puzzling about how all these things fit together.

formed when creating the world. Man was given free will by God so we can use that will to "image" the kind of creating that God did to make the universe. Of course, God has been known to "stiffen" a human neck on occasion; one particular woebegone pharaoh comes to mind. And so our freedom of will is not absolute, but subject to divine will. But from many other stories, we see that by and large, we're left to impose our will on the world as we choose.

Modern science is based firmly on Hellenistic principles.

Another Biblical premise is that man may use his free will to do wrong, then see what was wrong with the deed and repent. God will forgive.

What does divine forgiveness mean? It means that if you're sufficiently embarrassed, chagrined, and remorseful, then whatever dire and terrible forces you've set in motion will dissipate harmlessly rather than heaping upon your head all the pain and anguish you now see you so richly deserve.

Most of us who've lived more than twenty-one years have experienced divine forgiveness. Unfortunately, it's all too easy to learn nothing from the experience except that it's possible to get away with misdeeds. One could argue that some people are predestined to get away with things. But is that the only possible explanation? What is predestiny, exactly?

Predestiny means that when a person is born, or conceived, or begun somehow, there are conditions inherent in that beginning which predetermine in absolutely immutable form exactly what will happen to that person. None of the person's subsequent decisions *matter.*

This was one prevailing notion in Greek culture. The classic Greek tragedies are full of people squirming and struggling to avoid their destinies—but anyhow it all works out as foretold or decreed by the gods. *There is nothing you can do to change your destiny.* But do you really have one? And if so, where did it come from?

In this and many philosophical issues, the Bible is the absolute polar opposite to Hellenistic thought.

Yet modern Western civilization is derived from Roman civilization, which was heavily influenced by the Hellenistic philosophers. Modern science is based firmly on Hellenistic principles.[3] These philosophies and principles are what we absorb in the unspoken assumptions behind everything we learn in school, but most particularly in the methods of thinking necessary to get through school.

3. The Greek mathematicians such as Pythagoras, and the natural philosophers such as Aristotle, set down the principles of logical thought which are the unseen foundation of all modern science. Those principles work so well that they are rarely questioned, yet they lead to propositions at odds with the Biblical concept of reality.

Yet in Sunday School, we are enjoined to manage our lives according to rules and laws which are inherently antithetical to Hellenistic thought.

Small wonder most of us don't know whether a fortuneteller can or cannot foretell the future, but we firmly believe—without knowing why—that it would be either evil or stupid to take a fortuneteller's advice, while at the same time, we're excited by the idea of finding a good fortuneteller.

Let us work within the Biblical context here. Let us assume that we want very much to live according to the Biblical codes of behavior. So we must understand what's wrong with fortune telling. A good way to avert disaster is to understand what's wrong with an action so we can avoid it; then we won't need to earn divine forgiveness.

To get a firm handle on this, we have to consider bits and pieces of knowledge associated with a variety of disciplines, looking at a few references out of context in order to assemble an idea worth considering—not an ultimate truth, just an idea to think about and investigate later.

One group of disciplines is called variously the occult, or the esoteric sciences, or magick. (Magick with a final k to distinguish it from stage illusion.)

By magick I mean the philosophical system or view of the universe built on the assumption that reality can be shaped by the human will, mind, imagination, or emotion—that humans can take the reality that God created and create something out of it.

Obviously, by this definition, science is a branch of magick, for never has science denied the seminal role of the human mind and will.

However, any spiritual discipline that practices prayer is also a branch of magick—albeit a wholly different branch from science.

Science says that no matter what prayers, invocations, or incantations you say over a pot of chemicals, the result will be determined by the chemicals added and the conditions maintained, not by the emotional

Attempts to violate Natural Law don't work.

pitch and essential moral fiber of the chemist.

Magick says that the chemist's essential moral fiber is more likely to affect the result than any amount of meticulous lab technique.

In science, what you do is really all that determines the success or failure of an operation. In magick, who you are is what determines success or failure.

Within the framework of science, it is easy to take into account who the operator is—personality traits determine just how meticulous and repeatable a person's lab technique is, and emotional disturbances can cause lapses and mistakes. And so, science is a branch of magick, but magick is really much, much bigger.[4]

There are two basic kinds of magick, black and white. And then, of course, there are many shades of gray.

Everybody's heard of black magick, but how many people can really define it? What is it about black magick that makes it "wrong"? And why is it wrong?[5]

A good working definition focuses on one element that distinguishes black magick from white: black magick always involves the usurpation of another being's free will, the supplanting of one being's will with another's, or merely interfering with another's exercise of free will.[6] The white magician quite cheerfully pays any price to avoid hampering anyone's free will.

It takes a lot of practice to learn to apply this definition of black magick vs. white to real

4. How much bigger, we will see later when we discuss the structure of the Tarot deck, and where science fits into it.

5. We'll need a grip on this concept when we try to distinguish an expert Tarot reader worthy of trust from a fortuneteller or a charlatan to be avoided.

6. That being or other can be Nature or God. For example, controlling the weather for your own convenience usurps God's role and denies others their convenience. Anything that one does for one's own profit, convenience, or to avoid one's own discomfort, shades into the black when it fails to provide an equal profit, convenience or avoiding of discomfort to the rest of the universe as well. The easiest rule of thumb for practicing magicians to apply is never to use magick for personal gain. Following this rule avoids gray areas except where a do-gooder personality prevails.

world situations,[7] but let's try to apply it to our problem of why there is a Biblical prohibition against fortune telling.

Recall that the prohibition, as originally written, was against those who took money to tell people what was going to happen to them. Such fortunetellers were, by simply existing within the city gates, advertising the idea that a person's destiny is already determined and can be discerned—by certain, special people whose services can be bought.

That idea is inherently antithetical to the Biblical precept of free will and divine mercy because it neglects the person's ability to shape and mold his/her destiny from moment to moment by his/her decisions. It gets a person to dreaming of the glorious future which he/she has to do nothing to earn. Or it gets people struggling furiously to avoid an unhappy vision, acting on the prediction as if it were "real," thus failing to address their actual problems and likely bringing about the disaster they're trying to avoid.

That alone would be a good reason for a Biblical injunction against consulting a fortuneteller. But there's more. When something crucial is going on in a person's life, emotions intensify, fo-

7. For example, our legal system doesn't hamper anyone's free will. In order to live in the U.S. we all have given our free will agreement to abide by our constitution and laws. If we don't like it, we can mount a campaign to change the law or we can leave. Countries which do not allow citizens who don't like the law to change it or to leave are hampering free will.

cus, and peak, setting up an unusual state of mind. Most people, hustling into the city for an important business meeting, would be anxious, agitated. They would feel better, they tell themselves, if they just knew how it would come out. So they toss a coin to the cloud reader who tells them something.

In such a stressed state, they are suggestible, and the cloud reading takes root in the subconscious and manifests later as a self-fulfilling prophecy. These people have surrendered their free will control of their lives because exercising free will was too hard.

It doesn't take a psychiatrist to point out that this is a very bad strategy. The negative result may not manifest for years, but it will definitely involve a loss of self-esteem, and more than likely some form of self-destructive behavior. The more frequently the strategy is employed, the more destructive the final manifestation.

Telling fortunes is counter-productive.

Modern psychology and the lessons learned from the studies of battered wives and abused children show the tight correlation between repeated and habitual surrendering of free will and becoming dysfunctional in society and life.

A victim may have his/her free will beaten down by physical or verbal force, or he/she might co-dependently buy into the transaction. In either case, the result is a psychological disaster.

So going to a fortuneteller is counter-productive, even if the suggestion implanted by the foretelling is positive and to your apparent advantage. It is the fact that it is an implanted suggestion based on the concept of predestination that makes it negative.[8]

But what about the fortuneteller? Is it wrong to tell fortunes?

Going back to the definition of white and black magick, we can see immediately that the fortuneteller is in a lot of trouble. The act of saying to a person—especially one in a psychologically open and suggestible state—that their future is predetermined is an act of black magick because it superimposes the conscious will of one person on the subconscious will of another.

But, from within the Biblical point of view, it does something even worse than that.

God created the universe to function according to a set of rules and laws which He revealed to Moses. Taking all those rules and laws together, one can discern a coherent philosophy behind them. And that philosophy says that because humans have free will, and because God's mercy is there for the asking at any moment, any human being can repent and thus change

8. People go to hypnotherapists or spiritual counselors to have anti-smoking or other habit-breaking suggestions implanted. That's a different situation. First, the person has chosen to alter the habit. Second, no licensed hypnotherapist or counselor would attempt to predict a person's future or override their free-will choice.

their destiny in the flick of an eye.

The universe is constructed in such a way that your destiny is entirely in your own hands. No one can possibly predict your future. Not even you. Even an implanted suggestion, or a will destroyed by abuse, can be overcome at any moment by turning to divine mercy.

To foretell someone's future is to attempt to violate a Natural Law inherent in the substructure of the universe. A fortuneteller is smashing themselves against a brick wall with every prediction. The only possible result is a smashed fortuneteller.

So telling fortunes is counter-productive; going to fortunetellers is counter-productive.

Attempts to violate Natural Law don't work.

Another precept of magick is that the efficacy of the magician's acts is proportional to the amount of truth in his/her daily words—everyday utterances such as "dinner was delicious" and "I have a headache, Honey." Every tiny white lie erodes the magician's power. Since it is impossible to know a person's future, to predict that future is to lie. A fortuneteller very quickly becomes unable to get anything to work properly in their own life, never mind anyone else's.

So the Bible forbids fortune telling because it's impossible, and because it's black magick.

But does that have anything to do with the Tarot?

As I said at the beginning of this chapter, most people would agree that the Tarot is a tool of divination—but does divination have anything to do with fortune telling? What does divination really mean?

We're not dealing exclusively with dictionary definitions here. The dictionary has very little to do with how a living language is used within the mind of a native speaker thinking about a difficult subject. And it becomes even less relevant when we begin to include technical definitions from special fields.

In the field of magick, initiation means much more than just "beginning" and divination means something completely different from fortune telling.

Divination means seeing within, discerning the internal connections among mind, emotion, soul, and spirit. It means seeing the truth of a matter.

Divination is a discipline within the field of magick which can be taught. It doesn't require any special talent other than interest and an appetite for study and never-ending hard work. There's nothing much special about the Tarot as a divining tool. It's only one of many equally efficacious systems.

What a diviner does with the vision that has been divined is entirely a matter of that diviner's free will.

It is possible to use that vision for fortune telling. But by the time one gets very good at divination, generally one sees the idiocy of that.

So, discarding fortune telling as an option,

what's left?

Let's go back to Predestiny vs. Free Will. Predestiny was deeply entwined in the Hellenistic view of the universe, and Free Will is the basic premise of the Biblical view. But which is right? Which is correct? If one is correct and the other false, why do both linger on in the world hopelessly intertwined not only in our science and public morals but also mixed into a gray fog in our personal philosophies?

Think about it. Is this an either/or situation? Are these two philosophies actually mutually exclusive? To me it seems obvious that the answer is no. It isn't either/or. It's both/and.

In magick, there is an ancient Hermetic dictum, a principle abbreviated: <u>As Above; So Below.</u> It's an excerpt from a long document called the *Emerald Tablet of Hermes.*[9] It means that when one wants to learn something about what one can't see, one can look carefully at what one can see and extract the pattern. And the pattern will repeat.

In other words, the universe is constructed of basic patterns that repeat, or reflect into mirror images. When you've identified a basic pattern, you'll see it working out in different versions on different levels. This is the basic prin-

9. A study contrasting and comparing the text on the Emerald Tablet with the Qabalistic Tree of Life reveals haunting similarities, as if two seers or prophets from different ages and cultures had gotten a peek at the mechanism of the universe and come back to try to explain it to the rest of us. The explanations are wholly dissimilar, yet it's as if they both saw the same thing.

ciple behind the linguistic device called analogy.
Analogy will be used extensively in this book,
with the caution that, of course, an analogy is
never exact.

By analogy, we could study the laws of
physics to discover something about the laws of
karma.[10]

Consider the laws of Newtonian mechanics.
For example: a mass in motion tends to stay in
motion unless some outside force acts on it.

Suppose you are driving your car along the
highway and you come to an exit and find yourself on city streets. You're late for something important, and so you don't make that supreme effort needed to recalibrate your sense of speed
down to city street orders of magnitude. And
suddenly you're going 50 in a 25 mph zone, a
one-way one-lane street with cars parked on
both sides. A little child runs out from between
two cars right in front of your car.

By the laws of Newtonian mechanics, there is
no way that several tons of automobile is going to
stop in such a short space. And you hit the child.

Is that Free Will or Predestination?

Obviously, it's both.

You decided of your own free will, for

10. The Predestination vs. Free Will argument is an argument regarding the laws of karma—how is karma generated and dissipated? If
each person's destiny is predetermined, then there can be no karma
because what happens to a person is not the result of what the person
thought, felt, and did. If everyone has free will and can repent, then
there can be karma because one's current situation is the consequence
of specific actions.

whatever tangle of conscious and subconscious motives, not to slow down. After that, the laws of physics took over and predestined you to hit the child.

Also the child's free will, by whatever tangle of impulses, operated to bring the child out in front of the moving car at just the wrong moment. So it wasn't your free will alone that created the destiny.

In real life, it never is just one person's will. And there are always alternatives. In fact, most of us would elect to ram into the cars at the side of the street rather than hit a child. But sometimes we don't think that fast. Sometimes we don't react that fast. Sometimes we don't see the alternatives fast enough. Most of us don't debate these possibilities with ourselves when deciding whether to slow down upon exiting the highway.

But this is just an example to demonstrate how a decision made at one time can lock in certain results with immutable inevitability. Even though it's a free will universe, predestiny operates, but only so long as we don't change the original decision by another act of free will. In this case, the original decision was to get to the meeting on time, and the change could have been to ram into parked cars to avoid a child, thus giving up the meeting entirely...and possibly life itself.

As the laws of physics and the laws of psychology interact to create an accident "below," so "above" the laws of karma and the laws of psychology can interact.

Knowing this, and knowing how very much a psyche in motion will tend to stay in motion, a fortuneteller can indeed predict the future with uncanny accuracy. This can be very impressive and very convincing, but it also disregards free will and the "outside force" of God acting in the seeker's life.

The Bible takes no real definite stand on reincarnation, but the Jewish oral tradition that interprets the Bible doesn't rule it out. So let's look at how things would seem if we accepted reincarnation as a working hypothesis.[11]

Suppose, as some theories of reincarnation and karma attest, that before birth we each have a free-will choice about the circumstances of our birth. That choice is constrained by the laws of psychology.[12] Then the laws of karma take over and produce a destiny.

It is a destiny we have chosen of our own free will. So long as we don't do anything to change that original pre-birth choice or the psychological tangle of neuroses and lazy habits that dictated our choice, then nothing can change the destiny we're headed for in this life.

11. Jacqueline Lichtenberg has published 14 novels exploring a wide variety of theories of reincarnation and karma. For a list of availability send a self-addressed stamped envelope to P.O.B. 290, Monsey, NY 10952.

12. Keep in mind that we are only just beginning to discover the laws of psychology.

That destiny is there to rub our noses in the results of prior attempts to violate the laws of the universe.

In this life, we are predestined because we've used our free will to trap ourselves. If we could remember that pre-birth choice and the motives for it, we could choose to change our destiny.[13]

And now we come to a legitimate application of the diviner's art and the proper use of the Tarot.

When a Tarot reader gets to be very, very good at reading, sometimes the cards reveal that prenatal choice working out in a seeker's current life. Occasionally, a reader can discern some of the underlying tangle of neuroses and traumas, the baggage from past lives, that conditioned that pre-birth choice.

Seeing that past-life pattern and the connections between it and the decisions the seeker has made in this life is only half the Tarot reader's job, the smaller half. The larger half is explaining the patterns and connections to the seeker.

If the seeker can attain a receptive state of mind to hear painful words, and if the reader can find the least painful words to give the seeker a glimpse of that pattern, the seeker may—after some days, weeks, or months of hard work and reflection—discern just what was wrong with what they were doing, and be able to

---

13. Most people do have some memory of that pre-birth choice but it manifests not as a "past life memory" but as a mild aversion or affinity for certain people, places, or situations. Often such aversion or affinity is swamped out by present life experiences.

approach the Throne of the Creator of the Universe with all the shock, shame, consternation, and repentance necessary to evoke divine mercy.

If all these things can be accomplished, (and that is admittedly very rare) all bets are off about the seeker's destiny.

So no one well versed in the art of divination would ever dare attempt to or pretend to foretell anyone's future.

Well, if the Tarot is not about fortune telling but rather about finding a repentant approach to God, then why would anyone equate Tarot reading with devil worship?

Why Do Some People Equate Tarot Reading With Devil Worship?

You may have noticed that this book is laid out as a series of questions. Each question is discussed, and some of that discussion takes the form of proposed answers or hypotheses or working theories. But in no case— let me emphasize this—that in *no case* is the reader to take those answers, hypotheses, or theories as an answer to the question.

This is a discussion. The objective is to focus attention on the questions to consider before considering a Tarot reading. I'm not arguing my own philosophical stance; I'm presenting one stance for you to argue against to develop your strength.

Each of you must consider these questions and discuss them thoroughly within your own mind and/or with others. It isn't necessary, or even advisable, for each of you to come to the same conclusions. The point isn't to match your conclusions with anyone else's but to find out what you, yourself, think and feel. That's the first step to discovering whether you need a Tarot reading, and if so where and how to find the kind of reading you do need.

One of the issues you'll have to face when you search for a Tarot reading is the problem of the Devil. It's a problem that's stumped theologians for thousands of years, and I don't propose to solve it here. But neither can it be side-stepped. Would an adventure into the Tarot be for you an exposure to the Devil and all his temptations?

There are many people who should not tangle with the Tarot or any other divinatory tool. You might be one of them. Then again, you might not. How do you tell?

Well, you have to know what the Tarot is—and what it is not. You have to know something of the kinds of people who provide Tarot consultation and how to tell the difference between them. But mostly, you have to know a lot about yourself and something about the Devil.

Much information demanded in that previous paragraph lies in the area of the mind where most people fear to tread...and with good reason.

As a swamp, a rain forest, or a jungle can become utterly impenetrable when no one has kept the pathways hacked back, so too the slush at the bottom of the mind can become thick with undergrowth gone wild. *Things* live in that undergrowth. The longer it's left untouched, untraveled, ungroomed, the more the *things* flourish.

Stephen King is a master artist who knows just how to expose those things to the light of the conscious mind. A lot of people consider horror movies and books good fun. But others are just too deeply affected by them and don't enjoy looking that deep into the human psyche. People with either sort of attitude can come to a place in life where a Tarot reading could be beneficial. But there's another group that becomes fascinated by horror, fascinated and even obsessed.

Anything which promises quick, cheap but effective answers is truly dangerous....

Such people are at risk.

As you would hire an expert guide for a safari into the Amazon jungle, and that guide would hire local natives to advise him, so too any reasonable person planning a safari into the underside of their own mind would hire an expert wise enough to consult other experts. It's possible to get trapped down there and never get back.

The danger is especially acute for those

who have left those inner trails wholly untraveled. The older you are, the greater the risk. The more of a safari it becomes rather than just another trip to the corner grocery store.

But there come moments, turning points, when events in the outer world force people, even people at risk of obsession, to turn inward for answers. The less accustomed you are to looking inward, the more risky that journey is because during those years of neglect things have taken up residence in that swamp underneath your conscious mind.

The Tarot is an easily accessible tool for mapping that swamp. Its accessibility at every bookstore is part of what makes Tarot so dangerous, for it is a tool that requires a great expertise to handle. But the other part of what makes the Tarot dangerous is its apparent promise of answers.

Each encounter with the Tarot leaves a seeker with the impression that one more encounter will finally reveal a good, solid *answer*; that by just trying harder or longer, the seeker will discover information that will let them solve their problem easily and quickly, find the right thing to do to avoid all danger and finally triumph over their enemies.

We are a "10 Minutes a Day—Quick Weight Loss—Tax Computations Made Easy" civilization. Computerization of our society, from airlines to the stock exchange, is magnifying this human trait by nurturing and rewarding the expectation of instant, easy access to information and problem solving.

When we bring those expectations to the Tarot, we can get ourselves into more trouble than we ever knew existed.

What the Tarot cannot do is tell you something you don't already know. So why is it equated with devil worship?

Well, what *is* devil worship? And why is it wrong?

Biblically, the Devil is supposed to be a fallen angel who has chosen to rule in hell rather than be ruled in heaven. This isn't a book on theology, so we'll leave aside any discussion of what all that might possibly mean and what sections of the Bible it's derived from. (What those quoted sections actually say and what they really mean is a whole, huge Ph.D. thesis in itself, and not truly essential in the process of reading Tarot.)

What's wrong with devil worship is much easier to discuss. It's not the devil part that's so objectionable to the religions that follow the Bible. It's that worshipping anyone or anything other than the single One Who Creates and Sustains the Universe, the I Am That I Am, is against one of the Ten Commandments.

In other words, devil worship is idolatry. So it's a prohibited behavior, just like murder or adultery, and that prohibition doesn't depend on the nature of the Devil.

It doesn't take a Ph.D. in theology to grasp

that simple fact. The real knotty problem is whether you accept the prohibition against worshipping other than the Creator of the Universe, and if you do accept it, why do you accept it (i.e. because Authority has decreed it, or because you can see what it leads to and you don't want to go there? Or maybe because you know God and like Him a lot and are signatory to His Covenant).`

Now, if you don't have a problem with idolatry, you don't have to read the rest of this chapter. If you've grasped the problem with fortune telling in Chapter One, nothing you'd do with the Tarot would lead you into behavior you find objectionable...only dangerous.

But if you think idolatry is something you'd prefer to avoid, then some serious thinking has to be done before you tangle with the Tarot. And you could very well, and very wisely, decide never, ever to get near the cards.

So, how could the Tarot lead someone into idolatry?

It could happen, and it could easily happen without the reader knowing it was happening. A friend of mine has called such processes the "slippery slide to perdition."

So first we need a mundane, operational definition of the Devil, and then we have to discuss what aspects of the Tarot itself and what aspects of human nature combine to grease that slide to perdition.

Well, what does the Devil do? The Devil whispers in your left ear and lures you away from doing what you know is right, what you "ought" to do. The Devil says it's all right to gratify your every whim and desire. The Devil says that the proper use of power is to prevent yourself from feeling anxious, or from experiencing physical or emotional pain. The Devil says it

Tarot cards are just tools. To think of them as anything else is to tread danerously close to idolatry.

doesn't matter what harm you cause to others, it's your right to avoid suffering in any form. The Devil says you can have everything for virtually nothing—all he wants is your soul, and you have no use for that anyway. You don't even know where you generally keep your soul, you certainly haven't seen it lately. You'll never miss it. Just sign right here—a little drop of blood will do the trick (genetic printing, fool-proof identification)—and then you can have anything you want instantly and without cost. All your problems will be instantly solved.

Boy, doesn't that sound familiar? Didn't we just discuss above how the Tarot seems to promise easy instant answers that will solve your problems virtually free? ($12 for a deck and $6 for an instruction book.)

But is it the Tarot that promises to solve your problems? Or does that whispered promise, that seductive lure, come from somewhere else? Well, what aspect of human nature allows us to avoid emotional and physical pain? And how does that aspect work?

Any psychologist can tell you that neuroses are a pain-avoidance mechanism. The only way a young child has to deal with a world they can't understand, affect, or control is by shunting the pain aside, walling it off, burying it, and forgetting it. When in adult life that shunt becomes habitual, and the habit itself forgotten even while it functions, the shunt is called a neurosis.

It's healthy for children. It's a necessary

mechanism for maintaining sanity during the helpless years. But if, during the teens and twenties, you don't break into those little compartments of set-aside pain and take out all that old shock, bewilderment, bereavement, disappointment, etc. and feel the pain and deal with it, then during your thirties, your emotional responses will become progressively more inappropriate. You'll develop "buttons"—subjects where you are oversensitive, or "blind spots"—subjects you can't respond to at all. Even though you, yourself don't see your responses as inappropriate, your friends may.

Depending on the nature of the traumas hidden behind those walls of neurotic block, on the thickness of the walls and whether the walls have any other doors or windows into other parts of your psyche, and depending on your intrinsic sensitivity, a neurotic block (the same kind of neurotic block that every healthy person has in abundance) can become so thick and so isolated that the material behind it becomes a dissociated plexus.

Now we're beginning to talk about serious mental illness. A dissociated plexus can evolve into a separate personality. Or it can remain a minor annoyance that doesn't affect the person's ability to function in society.

But a dissociated plexus can become the seat of inexplicable compulsive behaviors, the kind of thing that you do even though you don't want to, but you can't stop and you don't know why. Often you conclude your inability to control your behavior is a moral weakness.

It might not be. In some cases, it's not a real mental illness either. But it's kind of like having a sore in the middle of your back: you've got to get somebody else to put medicine on it and dress it for you because you can't see it, let alone reach it. But oh, boy, do you feel it!

Well, what's all this got to do with a mundane definition of the Devil?

One way to understand the significance of The Devil card in the Tarot is as the material locked away behind neurotic blocks. Sometimes The Devil card represents the compulsive behaviors generated by mildly dissociated plexuses . The card can represent a human psyche dominated by the pain-avoidance mechanism rather than using that mechanism for soul growth.

That's nothing to do with fallen angels or evil incarnate; it's a non-theological definition of the Devil. It means we have to confront the idea that the Devil (our pain-avoidance mechanism) resides within us all. There's no escaping it as there's no escaping the omnipresent God.

But using this particular concept of the nature of the Devil, there's no confusing the Devil with God, and no temptation whatever to worship the Devil.

Using the above definition of the Devil, one can regard all evil behavior in humans as simple childishness. Consider the villains in the Superman movies. Look closely at exactly what they're doing and why and see if it doesn't remind you of your average three- or four-year-old holding a loaded gun and set on gratifying desires and getting away with it.

We said above that the Tarot is like a road map into the swamp at the bottom of the mind, a swamp in which *things* (neuroses and dissociated plexuses) live. Just around the next corner, just up the next bayou, lives the *thing* that has the answers we need. One more expedition and we'll find it and we'll force it to tell us how to solve our problems; then we can rule the world and the world will gratify our every desire instantly instead of forcing us to do things we don't want to do.

Get caught in that fallacy and you can start to look to the Tarot (or the places the Tarot leads you) to solve your problems.

What you look to or depend on to solve your problems is what you worship. That's what "worship" means, to regard something as so elevated above you that it can hand out life or death and you have no option but to accept. Therefore, you'd better stay on the good side of that power.

You start catering to that power, trying to bribe it into solving your problems for you, and you turn away from the real power, That Which Creates and Sustains the Universe and gives you free will with which to solve your own problems. This is idolatry.

Now, this is a true danger with the Tarot, yes,

but it's exactly the same danger as you face with science, technology, computers, doctors, lawyers, the law, courts, daddy, or whatever other element dominates your outer life and promises to alleviate or avoid physical or emotional pain...or dish it out when you fail to please.

Our overall civilization right now is in a condition of worshipping science and technology. Shovel enough sacrificial money into the maw of science or technology and it will solve the problems of disease, hunger, poverty, or the plague of depression sweeping our nation (evidenced by the suicide rate).

Since the prevailing civilization advocates idolatry, those who have decided to adhere to the Ten Commandments have a very hard time. It's small wonder they equate Tarot with devil worship. If you're looking for answers, the Tarot can get you into more trouble than you can get yourself out of—because it doesn't have any *answers*, just more questions.

Anything which promises quick, cheap but effective answers is truly dangerous, for you might get to thinking that now that you have a source of good, solid answers—Real Truth—and now you can handle things by yourself and you don't need God at all.

Is that what the Tarot is, a tool for circumventing the need for God?

Watching friends and neighbors tangle with the Tarot and go down in flames, reasonable people might well conclude that it is. They would quite reasonably conclude that there's no need to know exactly what the Tarot is, what it consists of, where it came from, and how and why it works in order to condemn it absolutely.

Would they be wrong?

What Are The Real and Present Dangers of Using and/or Learning Tarot?

What can we possibly learn by looking more closely at what the Tarot is, what it consists of, where it came from, and how and why it works? Would such a look reveal whether the tool or the user—or both or neither—should be condemned as too dangerous? Let's try it and see.

So what does it mean to "read" Tarot? What does a Tarot reader actually do? A good place to start is to examine a few Tarot decks.

Some stores have a display deck out for customers to look at, but this is not usual because such a handled display deck can't be sold. A Tarot deck is a personal item, somewhat like a toothbrush or underwear. An experienced Tarot reader wants a new deck sealed in shrink wrap.

Another good place to see Tarot cards is in the instruction books that are often sold under

Occult or Astrology in chain bookstores. Very often they have pictures of the cards along with discussions of their meanings. Each popular deck has many instruction books (often saying contradictory things) available.

There are encyclopedias of Tarot—big, expensive oversize coffeetable books—which have color photos of many decks, some of artistic or historic importance. Libraries sometimes have such books.

Many modern decks are published by U. S. Game Systems, Inc. in Stamford, Connecticut or New York, New York . They have a catalogue.

Even the most cursory foray will reveal that there are an enormous number of Tarot decks currently available, and the number grows almost daily. The variations between them are mind-numbing. However, the variants are of little interest except to the scholar and the expert.

The usual Tarot deck consists of 78 cards divided into two sections. One is the Minor Arcana, consisting of 56 cards in four suits (numbered 1-10 plus King, Queen, Knight, Page). The other is the Major Arcana, consisting of 22 cards. The Major Arcana is unlike any in a playing deck; the cards have names such as The Hierophant or The Hanged Man and are not part of any suits. On television, in the movies, and on novel jacket illustrations, Tarot layouts are typically shown using Major Arcana with portentous pictures.

Some readers read only with the Major

Arcana and others read only with the minors (and thus can get the same results with any full deck of playing cards.) However, the Major Arcana have gotten the most publicity because they seem so mystical and thus "must hold important answers." But the truth is that the Minor Arcana are much, much harder to master and are the main study for advanced students.

One of the big differences between decks is the artist's rendering of the cards. Art is an extremely powerful tool for evoking emotion and com-

Art is an extremely powerful tool for evoking emotion.

municating nonverbally, and since the Tarot is about emotions and the nonverbal part of the mind, art is an ideal avenue of penetration into the substance of the Tarot.

However, all that glitters is not gold. Just because a deck is beautiful or somehow mysteriously attractive or artistically inspiring, don't think it must be useful for doing what Tarot does best. Beginners need elaborate artistic help finding the pathways into the Tarot. The most experienced readers use the plainest decks with few or no pictures, just Hebrew letters, Sanskrit letters, and astrological, alchemical, or Qabalistic symbols. Such readers may use illustrated decks to help a given seeker.

Each card of the Minor and Major Arcana bears an ensemble of symbols hidden within the art which together represent the essential meaning of that card. The artist must have a knowledge of what those symbols are and just how much artistic latitude there is in arranging

As a doctor interprets X rays and a rabbi interprets ancients law, so does a Tarot reader interpret the meanings of the cards.

them. The positions on the card and the relationships of the symbols carry meaning.

Remember, human beings share an odd quirk: they tend to like things that aren't good for them. But you don't choose a Tarot deck because you like it or because it makes you "feel good." That's like gorging on chocolate before dinner.

Still, there's no reason that the essential working parts of a tool have to be ugly. We beautify those things we respect and cherish. And thus with the Tarot, a beautiful deck is chosen by a person who has beauty within and who lives with respect for the Tarot and all who gaze upon it.

So if you learn to read Tarot yourself, or go shopping for a Tarot reader, look around at what decks are available; a reader can be judged by the deck he/she uses.

Why is it important for the symbols hidden within the artistic pictures to be "correct"? What will a Tarot reader do with those symbols that makes the correctness matter?

Of course, no two readers are alike, no two do exactly the same things, and few know how they do what they do. Obviously, nobody really knows how Tarot is read or why it works. But here is one model that may help you create a model of your own. Ultimately, to succeed—in your search for a good Tarot reader or to be a good Tarot reader—you must build a solid mental model like this one...and revise it as often as necessary.

So, what are the Tarot symbols? Where do they come from? What makes them "correct"? Why do they work?

You're reading this page by virtue of symbols. Letters are symbols. They are an arbitrary convention, and they work because we all agree on their meanings.

The Tarot symbols refer not to sounds but to archetypes for the nonverbal structures and functions of the mind and emotions. When I teach Tarot, I call these symbols the "alphabet of the left hand." As with an alphabet, the individual symbols mean little. It's when you combine the symbols into "words" (e.g. a Tarot card) that you have communication. And if you misspell the words, you may miscommunicate the meanings.

The "correctness" of the symbols on the Tarot cards comes from our general consensus agreeing to the reference for each symbol and the "spelling" of each "word." Just like alphabets, there are many sets of symbols which large groups of people have agreed upon meanings for and which work to communicate in their languages.

And so you have whole groups of Tarot decks relying on the symbol systems from diverse cultures. There's an American Indian deck, and there are African decks, and Egyptian decks, and Celtic decks, and so on. Each is perfectly "correct" and useful to those who speak those languages– and pretty much useless to anybody else. For instance, it can be helpful to look for a Tarot reader who uses a deck in a language you "speak" natively.

So with all this variation, what is it about a Tarot deck that makes it a Tarot deck and not something else?

Well, a Tarot deck consists of 78 objects, identical except for distinctive markings. They have to be objects which can move together according to the laws of random chance (such as shuffling cards). And that's about it.

Of course, such a stripped-down basic deck would be of use only to the highest adept in the Tarot reader's art. Lesser beings need some sort of mnemonic or subconscious associative trigger embedded in the symbols. How

Each culture, however, expresses these archetypes in their own "dress."

those associations work within the human mind is a little different from how letter-symbols work to let us read words.

The symbols associated with abstract concepts and base human emotions are connected to what Jung called Archetypes. An Archetype exists on a level of abstraction where it is identical for all human cultures throughout all time.

Each culture, however, expresses these archetypes in their own "dress." Looking at a group of such expressed archetypes, a person not trained in anthropology might assume they were unrelated.

And so it is with the plethora of Tarot

decks on the market today. They look different, but they're really all the same. At least the ones that really are Tarot decks are all the same.[14]

So a Tarot reader must learn to understand 78 distinct ensembles of archetypal symbols before he/she can even start to read (156 if the reader reads reversed—upside down—cards). It must be that only the intellectual giants of our time, or those with eidetic memories, can become Tarot readers!

Actually, it's not that grim.

That would be like having to memorize the *Oxford English Dictionary* (unabridged) before tackling *Little Red Riding Hood*. All that's necessary to learn to read words is to understand that the little squiggles on the page represent sounds, and if you can kind of approximate the sounds the squiggles represent, you may recognize the word that your mouth almost formed, and so know what the words say.

To learn to read Tarot, you must understand that the Archetypes, expressed by arbitrary cultural convention in the symbols on the card, represent something as real as sound and as accessible. That something is emotion. You have to let yourself look at the symbol and feel

14. There are decks on the market with added cards because the artist didn't understand that you can't add cards (or subtract them) and still have a Tarot deck. Such decks can be used quite well for all the various functions of divination, so it's easy to assume it's the same thing. But there are a lot of very effective divinatory tools that have been invented by various cultures down through the ages, and many of them are in good use today. That doesn't make them Tarot.

the emotion, let it manifest in your nervous system as the sound manifests in your mouth when you learn to read a word.

Once it's manifested, then you have to identify it, find its root down in the quagmire of your subconscious and how it's connected to everything else in your life.

Now an analogy from music. Think of how a guitar string tuned to C can be plucked and make another guitar string tuned to C an octave higher vibrate even though they aren't touching. The air vibration alone transferred the energy to the other C string, but not to the E or D or any other string. (If you understand the why of this, you'll understand a great deal more from this analogy.)

People make mistakes. So do Tarot readers.

In magical theory, Archetypes reside on the astral plane as organized patterns that store the energy from each thought tuned to them. The Tarot is such an organized pattern, and each deck has its own area within the Tarot's zone on the astral plane, and its own frequency.

By concentrating on the symbol which *to you* represents a particular archetype, you "tune" yourself to the note of that archetype. (Prayer works the same way; you put yourself in tune with what you're praying to, and energy flows into you. Remember by our working definition of magick, discussed in Chapter One, prayer is a magickal exercise.)

Now, once you are tuned to the archetype, you resonate to that energy just as a guitar string resonates to other strings tuned to the same note. You can gain or lose energy via a medium that isn't apparent, just as air isn't apparent.

And so it follows that one should take great care in selecting the archetypes one attunes oneself to. Some archetypes drain energy ferociously. Others provide more than a given person can safely use.

Where does that energy enter a person?

Through the subconscious. Down in the bottom of the swamp are some hatches, doors into another reality—or so some magical theories hold. If you swim down through one of those doors, you'll go through a long tunnel and come up outside your own personal mind, in the Great Ocean, the primordial sea of the human collective unconscious.

Somewhere out there is God. He talks to us through the collective unconscious and the hatchways at the bottom of our personal unconscious. Depending on how much of a tangled jungle chokes our swamp, pure energy or God's messages may have a hard time getting through undisturbed.

And of course forest fires can still happen even in a swamp. Peat laid down over lifetimes (one karmic theory and some astrological ones claim that one brings some of the content of the subconscious along from past lives) can catch fire and smolder for eons, then burst into conflagration hot enough to burn.

A person with a charred, nonfunctional subconscious is a nonfunctional person, a mental vegetable. Even just a little destruction can mean debilitating mental pain or aberrant behavior.

And so again, we see the danger inherent in messing around with the Tarot, especially a badly chosen Tarot deck. A Tarot reader (whether an interested beginner or a more experienced reader) who has opened him/herself to a raw, unregulated, sudden influx of archetypal energy, without knowing how to deal with such manifestations, might begin showing signs of personality disintegration.

That disintegration might not be obvious, or at least not to observers. A person might seem quite normal but be riding a "slippery slide to perdition" in his life and quite happy to bring you along by reading Tarot for you.[15]

So how do you tell whether you want a particular person to read Tarot for you? There is a simple question you can ask yourself which ap-

15. When I teach Tarot, I use a more elaborate explanation of symbols and a much more detailed explanation of the dangers a beginning Tarot reader exposes him/herself to. Here, I have not even touched on the methods for avoiding those dangers, so please do not think to use this book as a self-teaching guide in the Tarot—not without many other sources and much training behind you.

proximates the risk. "Would I give this kind of person a key to my house?" Giving him/her a key to your mind is even more intimate. Is this the kind of person you would give a signed blank check to, a check to the biggest account you own?

One way to make such a judgment of a stranger (and you'll get the best Tarot readings from total strangers) is to look carefully at his/her Tarot cards and ask for an explanation of the meanings of the symbols. (When *you* are reading Tarot, be prepared to answer the same questions.)

How can this help? If you're a beginner, you're not about to become an instant expert Tarot reader yourself in order to judge whether they know the "right" answers or not.

Ah, but there are no "right" answers. Each answer, any answer, is acceptable.

A Tarot reader begins learning the cards not by memorizing a dictionary of symbols but by working with the symbols until he/she has discovered what each symbol means to him. This "mapping" of symbol meanings is personal, totally idiosyncratic. The reader must discover what symbols are connected through his/her own subconscious to which of the archetypes "out there."

But an evaluation of the meanings a reader has assigned to the Tarot symbols can't indicate whether that reader can give accurate readings. It can indicate whether another reader subscribes to moral and ethical codes in harmony with your own. It can tell you whether this person is trying to direct their life along a line that you think goes toward what you think life's ultimate goal and purpose should be. It can't tell you whether they're succeeding or not, only whether they're trying.

Another test for Tarot readers is to be asked why they chose this deck as opposed to another. It helps if you know the names of the decks. Very often, Tarot readers will tell clients that a particular deck is "very powerful" and gives dynamite readings.

An answer like that cannot be taken at face value. It's a kind of standard answer people who read for strangers have developed as a variety of brush-off, a way of saying, "this is too technical to discuss with a beginner." But there are others who really mean it.

You can distinguish by asking further questions such as, "Why would power be a factor?" "What is Tarot power, where does it come from, and how can you tell that a deck is powerful?" Or, "My problem is so common, I doubt any power is necessary to crack into it. Why don't we use a less powerful deck?"

Many people who have taught themselves Tarot or learned from a commercial teacher are learning Tarot as part of a program aimed at gaining magical "power." Most legitimate occult schools and orders automatically reject anyone who seeks to gain personal power as a result of their studies. So a person's attitude toward an understanding of occult "power" of various sorts (where it comes from and what it can be used for—and what it must not be used for and why) can reveal to you how they would use the power over your unconscious that you are about to hand them by seeking a reading from them. Or vice versa.

Let me sound one note of caution here. The search for a useful Tarot reader is not the search for a Perfect Person. In fact, if you could find one, a Perfect Person probably wouldn't be much use to you unless you're ready to become Perfect yourself.

The most useful Tarot reader will be someone who has just gone through something analogous to what the client is currently going through. Thus a few questions put to a reader about his/her life situation and stance would be useful to ask; age, occupation, marital status, schooling...the usual resume stuff that anyone would politely tell a stranger they were about to do business with. Don't volunteer anything in the area you wish to discuss with the cards (and ask a client not to do the same) but do probe for the situation of the reader in that area.

If the reader still has some ultra-sensitive buttons in that area, chances are you won't get anything useful from a reading with him/her.

But again, don't discard people just because they're not Perfect. People come in Small, Medium, and Large of Body, Mind, and Soul. They don't come in Perfect. Angels come in Perfect.

Besides, life isn't about doing things Perfectly. Life is about mastering error-recovery techniques. Otherwise, we wouldn't have been given brains that glitch out and put the hot coffee in the refrigerator and the milk carton back on the stove. People make mistakes. So do Tarot readers. It's not whether you make mistakes that counts. It's what you do about it afterwards.

But, knowing we must inevitably err, it is also incumbent upon us to minimize not only the frequency but also the severity of our mistakes, to develop fail-safes. Which brings us to the discussion of why so many Tarot readers refuse to take money for their readings.

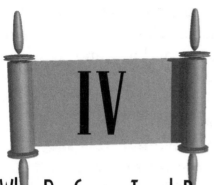

Why Do Some Tarot Readers Refuse To Accept Money Or Any Material Recompense For Their Readings?

Would a Tarot reader be more prone to make mistakes when getting paid for the work? After all, it makes sense that getting paid for something make you more enthusiastic about doing it right. Doesn't it give you pride in your handiwork? And doesn't it make you conscious of your reputation, so that you're less likely to get lazy and do a shoddy job?

If it gets around that you're doing shoddy work, who will offer to pay you better money? So getting paid makes you exceed yourself, and it builds your self-esteem.

Also consider it from the buyer's standpoint: "You get what you pay for." People are more likely to value what they pay a lot of money for. So it makes sense for someone who's offering advice to charge a lot for it so the advice will be accorded the respect it deserves.

Then why in the world would anyone work for free?

Well, there are a lot of answers to that, but it all boils down to this unresolved contradiction between the Biblical and Hellenistic philosophies.

Our civilization, our science, our technology, and a lot of our business practices rely on Hellenistic views of reality. Democracy itself is Hellenistic. The whole concept of majority rule is Hellenistic. The Romans elaborated on it, and the British did a good job transforming it into something the modern world could use.[16]

But our morals are Biblical. Our whole sense of right and wrong, and how to feel about it when you know you've done wrong, is Biblical.[17]

Most of the protections built into American law for the accused, and a lot of our notions of what constitutes evidence, are based in the Old Testament but stand at philosophical odds with the process by which we design laws.

This schizophrenic oil-and-water mix of

16. Don't forget Britain was once under Roman rule and a lot of British concepts of civilized behavior are basically Roman.

17. "Caveat Emptor" is from the Latin, a basic of Roman law, but very Hellenistic in origin.

There is a popular slogan you may see on buttons and bumper stickers that describes the problem a follower of the Biblical morality has with the Hellenistic theory of democracy as modified by the British and then by the American Constitution: Democracy is two wolves and a lamb voting on what to have for lunch.

The legal principles set forth in the Old Testament are designed to protect and nurture the rights and the sensibilities of minorities. Popularity doesn't empower you to implement your agenda.

philosophies reinforces the notion that *Money* (a Hellenistic value) is the Root of All *Evil* (a Biblical concept).[18]

Maybe Money isn't the root of *all* evil in any absolute sense, but because of the unresolved contradictions in our society's underlying philosophy, our Hellenistic attitudes toward possessions often prompt us to violate our Biblical ideals of behavior.[19]

Alvin Toffler, in his best seller, *Future Shock*, pointed out very graphically how industrialization, and its funding policies toward political elections (school boards are mostly politically elected or appointed officials), changed our school's curriculum—how each child is now cut and polished to fit into a niche, to mass produce employable people.

What parents could object to schooling that teaches their child to hold a job and become a

18. The Greek gods, remember, behaved toward each other and toward humanity in ways a follower of Biblical precepts would find either immoral or simply the result of a "dysfunctional family." Rape, incest, lust, kidnapping, betrayal, and substance abuse were the key themes of their stories. The Greek gods did not lead or inspire their worshippers to higher standards of morality. The Greek gods had to be bribed, circumvented, or hidden from. They were regarded as formidable enemies, not stern but forgiving parental figures.

19. Remember the Biblical stories commenting on human greed occurred to a people facing just the same philosophic dichotomy as the average American faces today. Both Old and New Testament are about God's efforts to separate off a people from the majority culture and imbue that people with a life philosophy in stark contrast to that of the surrounding culture (Egyptian, Babylonian, Greek, and later Roman). The stories are mostly about people who fall to the lure of the majority's values.

productive citizen?

And so there are certain things we all learn in school via what Toffler calls the covert curriculum. That hidden curriculum delivers one lesson Toffler doesn't discuss in depth. It's a lesson that awakens and reinforces an aspect of human nature that's always been there, but which is not lauded in a Biblical value system. That

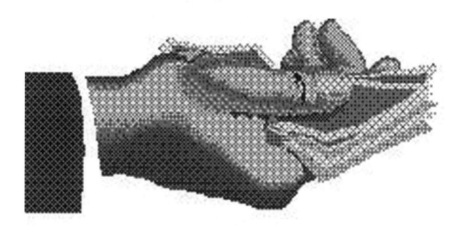

When readers are "hired," they are more likely to "perform."

lesson puts a Tarot reader in danger whenever he/she accepts money. It's a lesson about pleasing our superiors.

The Bible is full of stories about one man or woman standing against the majority and winning because they championed the morality God was teaching His people. In the Biblical morality, "I was just following orders," is no excuse if the orders come from a fellow human.

Anyone who's been through the American

public school system (and I'm sure it's very much the same in a lot of other countries) has been conditioned subconsciously via a covert curriculum—they never knew was there—to regard the person who signs their paycheck as the person whose will prevails. That person must be pleased.

On the job, you don't say, "I don't know if I can do this." Even if it's the truth, you don't say, "I don't know if I can meet this deadline." You don't make excuses. You don't shilly-shally around. You buckle down and get the job done, no matter what. And if you can't, you lie and make it look as if you did the job because looks are all that count. Under no circumstances may you tell the truth if the truth will displease those with power over your life.

Temporary workers know what I'm talking about. You have to *look* busy, even when you don't have anything much to do, because otherwise clients who come in might "get the wrong impression." Truth is not a value in the job marketplace.

No matter what, you don't discomfort the boss, the one who can fire you.[20]

So when you take payment (money or barter) you put yourself in the position of an em-

---

20. Remember the man who got fired for blowing the whistle on the O-Rings that caused the Challenger disaster? Millions of children took that lesson deeply to heart. Never tell the truth if it puts your job in danger. If we had a Biblical culture, that man would have been a celebrated national hero and the company would have been put out of business forever.

ployee, and all that subconscious conditioning kicks in.[21]

So, if you're a Tarot reader sitting across the table from a paying client looking down at a Tarot reading that makes no earthly sense to you, what are you going to do?

A lot depends on how much you need the money. If it should happen that you do this for a living and they're going to shut off the electricity if you can't make the payment—and your wife just brought home a newborn baby—you will be severely tempted to make up something. And you'll make up something that pleases the client.

Even without that much pressure, subconscious conditioning can make you genuinely see things in a reading that aren't there—simply to avoid the pain of violating a subconscious conditioning you'd swear isn't in you, or the conflict between the Biblical and Hellenistic philosophies you'd likewise swear isn't in you.

But by the magickal view of the universe, the results of that lie are the same as if you did know you were doing it and chose to do it. By magickal law, you are responsible for what your subconscious does when you're not looking just

---

21. This is, of course, one component in the abused wife syndrome. A "kept woman" has been subconsciously conditioned by her early schooling to please the one who hands out the meal tickets. It's also a component, one of many, in the famous defense of the indefensible, "I was just following orders." Both of these behaviors are deep and irreconcilable violations of the moral code required of those who follow Biblical precepts partly because they represent a surrendering of the Free Will to another human being.

as an absent dog owner is responsible for his dog biting the neighbor's kid. If you don't socialize your subconscious and keep it well leashed, you'll pay the consequences.

When you drain the swamp and tame the *things* lurking in your subconscious, your life comes together and starts to work. But when you feed the *things* that swarm in the swamp down underneath your mind, when you use them to avoid pain, they thrive and multiply.

The subconscious morass becomes thicker, more impenetrable, and the Tarot reader is less and less able to discern the information coming in from the Archetypes outside in humanity's Collective Unconscious—because that information has to bubble up through that swamp in the bottom of the mind. It gets distorted, obscured by noise.

So the reader has to make up more readings, and those lies feed the *things*—and so around and around.

As a result, there are a lot of Tarot readers who studiously avoid taking recompense in any form whatever. General wisdom has always said that a Tarot reader who takes money for a reading will lose his/her powers. I feel it's true.

But there are a lot who do read for money. Why? Should you avoid going to them for readings? Are they bad readers? Should you charge and would that make you a bad reader?

Ah, wouldn't it be a wonderful world if one simple rule would always work for everyone all the time!

But the human spiritual journey being what it is, what is right for one person isn't right for another. And what is right at one time in a person's life, isn't right at another.

So, sometimes, Tarot readers can quite legitimately ask for a fee and still give good readings.

Given the principle sketched above, how can this be?

I pointed out above that very often when a person sets out to learn Tarot it is as part (a small, vital part) of a journey of spiritual initiation. In many modern occult orders, passing classes in Tarot is an essential requirement for advancement. And it is required because certain sorts of spiritual advancement simply can't occur without mastery of some form of divination.[22]

So many who have journeyed alone have taken up the Tarot because they see it as a necessary adjunct to their training.

When one travels the paths of the spirit,[23] one is led inexorably to confront difficult and odious tasks. If there is something that is feared, it looms on life's horizon and must be dealt with. If there is something that is shunned or scorned,

22. Note that prayer alone is a form of divination. When practiced assiduously on a daily basis, sincere prayer does open up the pathways into the subconscious, clears out the underbrush, and accesses the gateways through which God's voice can be heard. Focused meditation on the Tarot is an extremely advanced form of prayer.

23. Karmic theory holds that such a spiritual journey is not appropriate or necessary in every single lifetime. Some lifetimes are lived to assimilate the results of previous progress rather than to break new ground.

8

"I'd never do a thing like that!" then one finds oneself doing it and learning to sympathize with those one previously scorned. If there is something lusted after, one gets it and discovers firsthand the truth about lust. And if there is something one prides oneself on, it disappears.

Thus, a Tarot reader who has been avoiding taking any sort of fee for decades might suddenly find him/herself destitute with no other recourse than to sell the one marketable skill they have left.

And in so doing, they must confront the temptation to pander to rich clients, to pride themselves on their reputations for uncannily accurate readings, to shroud themselves in the commercially successful trappings of the charlatan, to glow under the adulation of the ignorant.

If the person is committed to the Tarot as a path to enlightenment, then this is the ultimate test: to face the last few things skulking in the swamp, to drain it and make a lovely garden.

If passed, this test can forge a strength that will persist over lifetimes. If failed, the destruction can take dozens of lifetimes to overcome. Remember, by karmic law, one who wields power is responsible for the harm that power does. A Tarot reader who gives a false reading (even inadvertently) will encounter that seeker in another life and have to repair the damage done by the false reading. This can be a minor inconvenience, or it can cost a life. But that debt must be paid before further progress can be made. Or that's one of many theories about how karma works.

When money is involved, the silent contract for the transaction between reader and seeker is very different from when no money is involved. It's much easier to give accurate readings when no palm is crossed with silver. Later, when we discuss the Qabalistic theory of the Tarot and the Qabalistic theory of money, we'll see how money is in fact sacred, and when regarded as such, functions differently.

Here, though, we are discussing the search for an appropriate Tarot reader and what a Tarot reader ought to appropriately do. Unfortunately, there is no simple rule that can relate fee to quality in Tarot reading. You don't necessarily "get what you pay for." It doesn't cost the reader any more time or effort to read well than to read poorly. Higher and keener skills do not command higher fees.

The Tarot reader's skills are gained for the purpose of his own spiritual advancement, not for your edification. And so you can't pay him/her as you'd pay a doctor whose fees are set to compensate him for his years and years of schooling as well as for the fifteen minutes spent examining you.

So, if you find a Tarot reader who's right for you in your current predicament, or if you're reading Tarot at a commercial event, how do you decide what would be an appropriate fee? How do you decide if the charge is too high? How do you know if the charge is too much and is therefore likely to be on the "slippery slide to perdition"?   Or might the reader be considered a charlatan who's just pretending to read Tarot?[24]

Biblical philosophy provides a rule of thumb which is accepted in most magickal circles. As with the rabbis and rabbinic scholars, it is perfectly legitimate to charge for one's time, but not for one's knowledge of the sacred.

If you're buying or selling a fifteen-minute reading, how do you decide how many dollars that represents?

I could give a number, but that would make this book obsolete before it hits the presses. So I'll give you a formula. One consideration is minimum wage. Consider the going rate for an hour of unskilled labor. Since you're not paying for skill but for working time (time taken away from a person's ability to work for a living), minimum wage is a good rule of thumb. It's the least you are ethically bound to offer (or ask for) when you take time away from a person's work day.

But we all know that minimum wage has been politically jiggered around with until it doesn't represent a living wage any more. So the other factor in your formula is how much you make per hour. (Or how much the wage earner who supports you makes.) That is the maximum to pay for a reading.

24. Note that charlatans might produce extremely accurate readings, too, for they might have other sources of information— some of which are more impressive than anything the Tarot can actually do.

You can be comfortable paying or asking any figure between those two, though you may be fueling a Tarot reader's taste for rich clients. A good maximum would be the wage of a good mechanic, truck driver, or construction worker.

Americans don't like to barter. We're much more comfortable in a store with price tags, knowing just what a thing costs and knowing that if we want it, that's what we have to pay. And so the practice (especially at psychic fairs where most people get their first Tarot readings) is for the reader to put up a sign, usually something equivalent to "$5.00 for fifteen minutes."

But if you're looking for the most seriously dedicated students of the spiritual disciplines, they are unlikely to be at psychic fairs or in "Palmistry and Astrology" storefronts. They are more likely to be a friend of a friend. You'll find that they will agree to accept whatever you feel the reading was worth to you after the reading.

Very often, if you offer money to a reader who doesn't want to take a fee, they'll suggest you make a donation to the charity of your choosing. This is in accord with sound magickal practices, for in magick the giving of charity is as vitally important an obligation as it is decreed to be in the Old Testament.

One question that can be asked of a reader who is set to take a fee is, "How long have you been reading for a fee?"

Someone who finds that spiritual advancement lies through a period of reading for a living generally finds that it is a very temporary thing. As soon as he or she has successfully negotiated the dangers, other avenues open up and they eagerly leave the commercialization of Tarot behind them.

Using the other questions we've suggested in previous chapters, you can make an educated guess whether you or another reader might be descending that slippery slide to perdition or have just encountered some hard slogging on an upward path.

Yes, I said "guess." Ultimately, that's all you'll be able to do. That sounds as if I'm expecting you to be more psychic than Tarot readers are supposed to be.

Which brings us to our next question. What is the role of ESP in Tarot reading?

Does Learning To Read Tarot Make A Person Become Psychic? Or Can Only Psychics Learn To Read Tarot? Or Does Psychicism Have Nothing To Do With It?

What does "psychic" mean? What is ESP (extra-sensory perception)? Where does it come from? What is it good for? Does it even exist?

Those are questions to which you have to discover your own answers. But here is a theory that harmonizes with the view of the universe inherent in the Tarot. (There are, of course, others views equally harmonious. The point, I can't repeat often enough, is that I'm not arguing for a point of view but presenting something for you to argue against.)

The scientific establishment has not yet acknowledged the reality of ESP phenomena. None of the evidence presented for telepathy, clairvoyance, precognition, etc. has ever fully satisfied the scientific criteria for the conversion of a hypothesis into a theory.

All of the education available through public schools and universities in this country, all the "formal" education, is carefully designed to inculcate into students the scientific view of reality. It's a powerful and effective view that has transformed the face of this planet, lengthened our lives, and eased our deaths. If you want to hold a job in this world, you'd better master the knack of thinking within the scientific world view...even if you don't believe it.

And so we come to another one of those very difficult contradictions between the Hellenistic view of reality and the Biblical view.

In the Biblical view, the human spirit is a very real and potent force in the shaping of reality and is the determining factor in the outcome of any endeavor.

In the scientific view of reality, there is no evidence for the existence of a human spirit, never mind a soul.[25]

ESP is the term science has coined to designate a hypothetical set of senses through which the world is perceived: extra-sensory perception—note the Latin roots to those words. "Psy-

---

25. In one famous experiment, there was a recorded difference in the weight of a body before and after death, supposedly the weight of the soul, but that experiment hasn't been found to be reliably repeatable, which is one of the key criteria for converting a scientific hypothesis into a theory.

ESP does not make someone special or omniscient. It's just a talent which can be used or misused.

chic" is an older (Greek) term.

The scientific term avoids incorporating any indication of the origin of these senses. The older Greek term popularized by charlatans indicates that the origin is in the psyche (root of psychology, and also a Greek goddess who personifies the human soul, spirit, or mind).[26]

26. Note the Greeks had a problem with their culture's philosophic split between a mystical view and a mechanistic view, too. We inherited that split and have done nothing to resolve the conflict.

Both terms refer to something that not everyone has experienced. The scientific term ESP attempts to strip the mysticism out of it by eliminating the reference to a goddess. The older term imbues these rare experiences with the aura of a deity's blessing.

Which one is more appropriate?

Maybe neither....

Each term makes the person who experiences this odd type of sensory input into something unusual. Each term reflects its culture's attitude toward the *unknown*. In science, the unknown is regarded as something which, if real, can become known. In mythology, the unknown is unknowable unless some god or hero wills it, as Prometheus stole fire from the gods.

When looking for a usable theory (not truth, just a good working theory), it's always a good idea to regard prejudices with a jaundiced eye. The idea that ESP/psychic talent makes someone special is just such a prejudice. The idea that since we have failed to "prove" ESP is real, then it's probably not, is just such a prejudice. The idea that the unknown is unknowable is another prejudice.

Why can't science prove whether ESP exists or not?

This is not a Ph.D. thesis in psychology, so I'm going to sidestep the experiments and how the subjects have been caught faking results. We're trying to discover the role of ESP in the use of the Tarot so we can determine whether a psychic is a better Tarot reader—or maybe a worse one.

Science can't prove whether ESP exists or not because science is committed to objectivity and the "reality" of objectivity. ESP belongs to the realm of subjectivity and the "reality" of the subjective. Science is committed to the precept that subjectivity is unreal because it's not repeatable. Magick regards repeatability as *prima facie* evidence for quackery.

Learning Tarot doesn't "make" a person psychic.

In the Hellenistic view, as we said earlier, it's what you do in an experiment that counts, not who you are. Think of Pythagoras measuring triangles. Does it matter who measures the triangle or is an equilateral triangle an equilateral triangle regardless of who measures it?

In the Biblical view, it's who you are that counts, not what you do. If you need an equilateral triangle, it will be an equilateral triangle. Moses needed water in the desert; he hit the rock with his staff, and out came water. Never mind there's no water in desert rocks, and if there were water in the desert rocks, hitting the rock with his staff wouldn't get it out. But this was Moses so the water is wherever it is needed, even though he didn't follow his instructions precisely.

Thus, in the Biblical view, who you are is a function of all you've decided and all you've experienced, most especially repentance, forgiveness, and acceptance of divine orders. The first time you do something, it has an effect on you, so you are no longer the same person.[27] The second time you do that same something, you have to do it differently to make it work for you because you are not the same person who did it the first time.

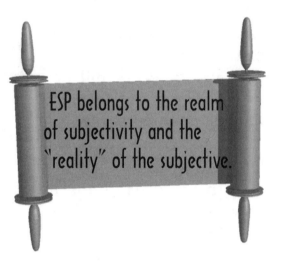

ESP belongs to the realm of subjectivity and the "reality" of the subjective.

It's enough to drive a scientist mad.

So here is a theory of ESP that is in harmony with the Biblical view, and at total odds with the scientific view.

ESP senses aren't "extra" at all. They're the senses of the soul and the spirit; they're the mechanism whereby the spirit communicates with the soul and the soul with the body.

Given that hypothesis, it follows that every single human being has these vital senses.

Well, that's obviously a false hypothesis,

27. Innocence protects, and absolute innocence protects absolutely. Innocence is not the same thing as doing something inadvertently because of a kink in your subconscious. That kink got there as a result of lost innocence.

then, because most people go through life without ever having a psychic experience.

Ah, but shouldn't one look very, very carefully at "obvious" conclusions before relying on them? "Obviously" the world is flat. Anyone can see that. Let's check out this one about ESP.

Let's go back to modern psychology's concept of the subconscious[28] and my analogy of the swamp with *things* living in it, and the magickal theory of the portals in the subconscious that lead to the Great Sea and ultimately to other planes of reality.

If psychics use the senses of the soul and spirit, then the sensory "organs" are those portals buried under the muck in the subconscious.

Considering the amount of muck most of us carry around, it's hardly surprising that conscious awareness of psychic experiences is as rare—and as repeatable at will—as spiritual conversion.

Thus, long, hard hours spent working daily with the Tarot, draining the swamp and socializing the resident *things*, should make it easier to find and open those portals—to open the psychic eyes and ears.

So learning Tarot doesn't "make" a person psychic, it just does the preliminary work neces-

---

28. Note that the Chinese do not accept the existence or reality of subconscious or unconscious. They describe the mind in terms of yin and yang, positive and negative. This reasoning, however, can work just as well if one half of the mental polarity is clogged up with detritus. Yoga and the Oriental Martial Arts use the yin/yang theory to spark off the same kind of spiritual growth that Western Mystery schools induce.

sary to access the psychic senses. It clears the scrub brush and maps trails.

Yes, preliminary work. Consider what it would be like to have your eyes taped shut at birth and then suddenly opened at the age of twenty or thirty. Do you think your eyes would focus, track, and see properly? Would your brain centers be instantly good at interpreting the information gathered?

So a person who's gained psychic experiences by working with the Tarot may not be reliable at interpreting those experiences any more than someone who's always been psychic would necessarily have no distorting muck to clear out.

The job of the Tarot reader is merely to become a conduit...

And there is another problem this model instantly points out. If the psychic senses are the senses of the soul and spirit, and the debris is cleared away so the portals can be opened (they might be rusted shut, you know), and information flows in from the other levels of reality Out There, and the soul gains some information...that doesn't guarantee that the soul will be able to communicate that information in undistorted form to the conscious mind.

Remember, our conscious minds have been

trained in the Hellenistic view of reality. Filtering information through that opposing philosophy—not to mention trying to hear anything over the cacophony set up by the remaining *things* jabbering about the newly opened portal—doesn't give us much of a chance of getting the message straight.

I said above that people don't come in Perfect, and a Perfect Tarot Reader wouldn't be much use anyway. The same applies here. A "straight" message might make even less sense than a heavily filtered one because after all, all our swamps contain related species of *things*.

The trick in getting from someone else a Tarot reading that can do some good is to pick a reader whose filters are pretty much like yours, but just a little different in the area where you need help. So people who commonly have psychic experiences at will are not necessarily better Tarot readers than those who are not conscious of their psychic faculties.

Heavily filtered psychic information can get in the way of giving a good reading. If the muck in the bottom of the psychic's mind is thick, he/she would do better to read only the patterns in the layout of the cards and compare them to the value system inherent in the Tarot. That alone can give the seeker all the contact he or she might want with the realities on the other side of the portals of the mind.

The job of the Tarot reader is merely to become a conduit through which the seeker can draw forth just the clues he/she needs without being confused by everything else the Tarot reader knows. Or in the analogy I sketched in a previous chapter, the Tarot reader can hold up a mirror that allows the seeker to see the sore on his/her back and judge its nature for him/herself.[29]

The object in a Tarot reading is to bring the seeker to a better grasp of the map of his/her subconscious and the connecting roads between the subconscious and his/her outer life.[30] This doesn't require psychically obtained information.

It does require a theory of how the soul and spirit are part of reality. That requires an elaborate visualization of the macrocosmic all—an understanding of the structure of the universe, a cosmology and cosmogony all built around an integrated philosophy with no contradictions left in it. In other words, it requires a theory of real-

29. This is only the first lesson in how to read Tarot, so we won't go into the methods of learning how to pull off this improbable trick here. Suffice it to say that the methods for learning this technique have been well developed by many schools of magick and all legitimate religions. It does not depend on what the Tarot reader knows but rather on how accurately they can set their own state of mind. A good Tarot reader works first in the state that produces alpha brain waves, and sometimes descends even into theta waves, as well as half a dozen states in between. These are known collectively as trance, but trance alone doesn't guarantee a Tarot reading will produce useful results for the seeker.

30. For an example of a connection between the subconscious and the outer life, consider someone who is their own worst enemy, but can't see it and believes that everything that goes wrong is someone else's fault. The subconscious shapes life, but seeing how is very hard when it's your subconscious doing the shaping.

ity in which there is no contradiction between the dictates of science and magick or between science and religion.

The Tarot is constructed around just such an integrated philosophy. It describes the connections between everyday reality and the realm of the spirit.

Do you need to know the philosophy behind the Tarot?

The Tarot isn't the only tool that can map the territory of the subconscious and the roads to the outer world. But by exploring the way Tarot resolves the science/religion conflict, and by comparing that resolution with your own stand on the matter, you can decide if the Tarot is the right tool for you.

Do The Principles Behind Tarot Defy Science?

I f you read the last chapter all the way through, you know my personal answer to this question is no. However, that might not be *your* answer.

So let me present the theories that I have evolved over the last twenty-five years of working with the Tarot as student, teacher, and practitioner, with just one cautionary note. No matter what theory of the Tarot you subscribe to, the practice of Tarot is totally idiosyncratic.

Your theory is likely to work better for you than anyone else's theory. It isn't a question of finding The Truth, or The Right Theory that can stand up to peer review, as in the objective world of science. It's a question of finding the most appropriate theory for you, now, and letting that theory evolve as your own understanding of the universe evolves.

There are so many decks, so many practitioners working Tarot for so many different reasons, all using different theories of how and why the Tarot works (not to mention what it is and where it came from), that very few Tarot readers may accept the theory I'm presenting here. And their lack of acceptance wouldn't prevent them from reading accurately.

So I'm going to give you a jumping-off place, just something to get you started developing your own theory. But please don't stop thinking, don't stop asking questions. And do maintain a healthy skepticism about whether the Tarot works or not, at least until you've seen it work.[31]

Scholars are still in disagreement about the origin of the Tarot. Since the one distinctive feature of Tarot cards is the pictures, one major source of information on its origin is Art History. The earliest known cards date from, I think, around 1390 and, as I recall, Art Historians can see Italian influence in the artistic renderings.

Earlier than that, we have no concrete data. In the 18th and 19th century, in the drawing rooms of high society, psychics became very fashionable. A number of charlatans used the Tarot as a mysterious tool. They wrote books about it, purportedly based on Ancient Egyptian writings (which were becoming popular as archeology started to become a science).

The educated of Europe were still working

31. That wouldn't constitute scientific proof, of course, since "seeing it work" is a subjective experience which doesn't count when proving things scientifically.

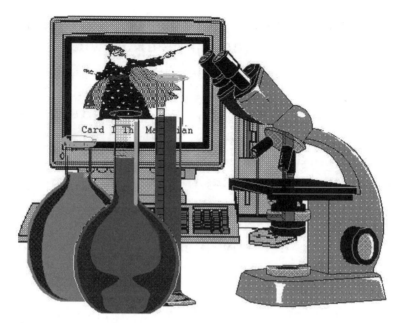

Tarot does not defy science, but rather science is a special case of Tarot.

on the Renaissance feeling that there had been a long-ago Golden Age during which all kinds of skills and "great wisdom" had been known and then lost during the Dark Ages. So imputing a manuscript to an ancient writer or source shrouded it in a mystic aura of High Truth. If it was old, it had to be much better than anything modern.

The idea that the cards came from Egypt became popular because they were known to be used by gypsies and "everyone knew" gypsies came from Egypt. After all, that's why they were called gypsies.

Today, linguistic analysis has identified the Romany tribes that turned up in Europe around 1400 as having left northern India a good many centuries previously.[32] They are as much Egyptian as Native Americans are Indian.

So did the Tarot come from India? Or was it picked up along the way? Nobody knows. Scholars think modern playing cards had their origin in Tarot cards, but that's not provable either. Consider that, before the printing press and woodcuts, the only way to make a Tarot deck was to hand paint each card. No two decks would be alike so it's improbable any given version would survive.[33]

Qabalah is the sum total of all Jewish mysticism.

One of the charlatans wrote that the Tarot was originated by the mystics of the 14th century. The Tarot, it was said, was their tool for communicating about alchemical and other esoteric subjects despite the vast linguistic differences between them. Another theory was that the mystics used the Tarot to hide their great secrets so they wouldn't be lost when the witch burning began.

Well, those mystical scholars really ex-

32. Research is divided on where they spent the intervening time, but their language had drifted considerably.

33. And that's the way modern students in magickal orders learn Tarot. They have to make their own meditation deck.

isted. And they did come from many different lands. And they did have a famous convocation in Marrakech, Morocco. And the Inquisition ripped those mystical schools to shreds. But did those mystics have anything to do with the Tarot? Nobody knows.

All investigations go back just so far, and then hit a brick wall or a fog bank.

The physical origin of the Tarot may never become known. Does that matter?

Possibly not. Let's work the problem backwards. Let's not start with some proto-Tarot deck and work out the derivation of the modern Tarot. Let's look at the modern Tarot and derive what the prototype might have been, then see if anything older than 1390 matches it. That may tell us more than any charlatan's glamorous theory.

As mentioned above, there are 56 Minor Arcana and 22 Majors. Of the 56 Minors, 40 are numbered cards such as you find in any playing deck. Sixteen are court cards. That is the structure of the Tarot deck. So what else is like it?

Now we reach way out into left field and pull in a bit of knowledge from a very esoteric discipline called Qabalah.

The origins of Qabalah are likewise shrouded in the mists of antiquity. Likewise, in the 13th and 14th centuries, it was imputed to the most ancient sources, as was the custom to give it a legitimacy no modern discovery could have.

This is not a textbook on Qabalah, so I'm not going to argue which legend might be more accurate, or which Qabalistic school is the more authentic. I'm just going to present one concept from that body of learning that happens to support this theory of Tarot.[34]

Qabalah is sometimes said to be part of the oral tradition received by Moses at the same time as the Torah (the first five Books of Moses). Qabalah contains the necessary key to understanding those Books.

The mystical roots of numerology are a small part of the whole Qabalah. Each letter in the Hebrew alphabet doubles as a number. That's how they did arithmetic and accounting before 0 (zero) was invented. So numbers are words, and words are numbers. Thus the Torah might be thought of as the "machine code" of reality, the program that is the operating system of the universe. Qabalah is the manual that comes with it.

But not a word of Qabalah was written down until, well, it's a matter of scholastic debate when the first Qabalistic texts were transcribed. It might have been around the time of the Babylonian Exile, or it might have been in the 12th and 13th centuries. Qabalah is the sum total of all Jewish mysticism, and a lot of it is shrouded in secrecy because it's regarded as dangerous.

---

34. Actually, I derived my theory of Tarot from the Qabalah, not the other way around. But the reasoning works both ways.

What has this to do with the Tarot?

By some odd coincidence, the main glyph or sigil by which all Qabalistic wisdom is organized (something roughly equivalent to the Periodic Table of Elements to chemists and physicists) has exactly the same structure as the Tarot deck.

How might this have come about?

Well, if there is some sort of Objective Reality out there, and mystics have been able to go out through the portals of the subconscious into that other reality and take a peek at the machinery of the universe, then regardless of which culture or time the mystic belonged to, the picture or image he/she brought back would bear a striking resemblance to that brought back by every other mystic who made the trip.

On the other hand, maybe those who developed the Qabalistic glyph knew the people who invented the Tarot?

Or maybe the people who invented the Tarot found some old Qabalistic manuscripts?

Or maybe it's just a random coincidence.

Or maybe the Tarot was invented by psychics reading the minds of the Jewish mystics who thought they were working in secret?

Does it matter how it happened? Does that affect whether the Tarot will work and what its underlying philosophy is?

It might. Remember the problem we've been having with the Hellenistic and Biblical views of reality. To figure out what the underlying philosophy of the Tarot is, we have to figure out whether it's Hellenistic or Biblical. Merely knowing that it resembles a Jewish mystical device doesn't tell us which tradition it belongs to, because Jewish scholars embraced Hellenistic

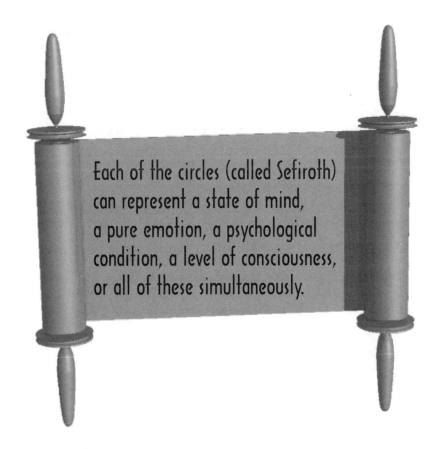

Each of the circles (called Sefiroth) can represent a state of mind, a pure emotion, a psychological condition, a level of consciousness, or all of these simultaneously.

thought during the same period when the Tarot appeared and when Qabalah was written down.

So we have to look very closely at the Qabalistic glyph called the Tree of Life, which is the Qabalah's organizing chart. Can we find something in that Qabalistic glyph that admits to the reality of the soul and spirit and their efficaciousness in determining the success or failure of any real world endeavor?

Take a good look at the color painting of the Tree of Life on the cover of this volume, and imagine how the Major Arcana fit onto the 22 pathways. In your mind's eye place the numbered cards on the circles and the Major Arcana neatly onto the pathways connecting the circles. Note that there are twenty-two letters in the Hebrew alphabet (Hebrew vowels are not properly considered part of the alphabet) and each one is assigned to a path connecting two circles.

Each of the circles (called Sefiroth) can represent[35] a state of mind, a pure emotion, a psychological condition, a level of consciousness, or all of these simultaneously. The connecting pathways are the transitions between these states of mind, and the cards laid on those pathways represent the mystical initiations that give one access to and control over those emotional states — i.e. that clear the neurotic blocks associated with those emotions, that make friends with the *things* living in the subconscious ooze.

---

35. CAUTION: I'm oversimplifying and giving you my own, personal layman's thumbnail explanation. There isn't a practicing Qabalist anywhere who would wholly agree with me, but these ideas would set off a heated discourse that would last into the wee hours!

For example,[36] someone going through the mystical initiation represented by the Tower might start out with an insufferable sense of invulnerability, of knowing what they're doing, and then suddenly, without warning, have their house burn down. That's right, "mystical initiation" isn't limited to the symbolism of ceremonial magic. The initiations that produce true adepthood are life's own experiences lived through one day at a time and either conquered or succumbed to.

On the other hand, the Tower card in a reading can simply mean that a $5.00 check you deposited will bounce through no particular fault of the check writer. The Tower refers to how it *feels* when something you *think* can't go wrong does, not to *what* can go wrong.

The event may be trivial or pivotal. The Tarot reader may not be able to tell which because it doesn't matter. What matters is the challenge the Tower represents to the state of mind cultivated by the scientific view of reality that assumes the results of an action are deter-

---

36. Advanced Tarot readers derive the core meanings of the cards from the very abstract meanings of the related Sefiroth. In the case of The Tower, the Sefirah on the reader's left looking at the diagram is #8, Hod, associated with science and ceremonial magic, while the one on the right is #7, Netzach, associated with color, sound, motion and especially the emotions surrounding victory, most especially the illusion of victory, i.e. "The Glory of War." Astrologically, Hod is associated with Mercury, the mind, and Netzach with Venus, the emotions. The Tower represents the rude awakening to the importance of the mind or the emotions, whichever you've been ignoring. This is an extremely healthy experience, but most artists use dire imagery on The Tower.

mined by the action, not by the morals and emotions of the actor. Or the challenge to the state of mind that assumes "love conquers all," that emotion is more important than facts. The event, of whatever magnitude necessary to deliver the message, will say that mind and emotion must be integrated, balanced, harmonized, and each must be regarded as sacred.

In my experience, all the Tarot cards, Major, Minor and Court, can be interpreted most elegantly via the Biblical view of reality, affirming the immortality of the soul and describing its internal circuitry and its "user interface."

In my experience, in a Tarot reading, interpretation depends on who the reader is.[37] It matters if the reader is a habitual doom-and-gloom crier or habitual optimist, but the reader's theory of how and why the Tarot works matters too.

So, how does the Tarot work? Assuming

37. Identity is an esoteric concept beyond the scope of this book. (For further information see my January through December articles for 1996 for my monthly book review column in the Internet magazine, The Monthly Aspecterian. On your browser type the URL http://www.lightworks.com/MonthlyAspectarian/index.html then point at the appropriate month and then Science Fiction by Jacqueline Lichtenberg.) Here's one way to look at it. You are the sum of all your experiences over all incarnations. Experiences are not just what happens to you, but the choices you make. Thus identity isn't a matter of luck or chance any more than a body builder's muscles are luck or chance. Identity is the result of the cumulative exercise of your Free Will—you are who you've chosen to be. That idea gives you full control of and whole responsibility for, your identity. As a corollary, you can't be envious or jealous of another person's position in life because they have nothing they don't deserve and nothing which you can't also have. (You might be jealous or envious of other things, but not of the things they have because of who they are.)

that mapping the Tarot onto the Tree of Life means that the Tarot works like the Tree of Life gives us a starting place into a vast body of knowledge, theory, and conjecture.[38]

Then what does this Tree of Life glyph represent?

Now this is my personal answer, not the answer of practicing Qabalists today.[39]

The Tree of Life glyph can be drawn dozens of other ways than the way presented in the color painting on the cover. Consider that the Tarot deck is just a Tree of Life glyph that's been cut apart into pieces. The markings on the pieces allow it to be reassembled.

The Tree of Life is to the budding science of psychology what the concept of the atom was to the science of chemistry, or the phoneme to linguistics. The single pattern with ten circles and twenty-two paths is the smallest indivisible unit of *something*.

The nature of that *something* is a matter of conjecture.

---

38. Tarot students spend a lifetime on it, but this book is about Tarot reading and readers, and interpreting their interpretations, not about learning Tarot, so this is only a very bare sketch.

39. By the way, "Qabalists" come in three main varieties today. There are Jewish Qabalists who write and publish works written either in academic English, clumsy English, or Yiddish and Hebrew. But they won't talk to you. There are Christian Qabalists who study Qabalah because it's likely Jesus studied some of it. Lots of what Jesus promulgated bears the mark of Qabalah. And there are neo-pagan Qabalists who are using Qabalah to sort out theories of ceremonial magic and to equate god-systems. And then there's me.

Since the Bible begins with a story of creation and continues with a chronicle of the relationship between God and His Creation and Creatures, and since Qabalah is supposedly the key to understanding the first five books of the Bible, maybe the Tree of Life glyph has something to do with the relationship between God and Man. But what?[40]

Well, Qabalists talk about energy propagating down the pathways of the Tree, filling up the "vessels" represented by the circles, and overspilling to carve the next channel, generating and filling up the next "vessel."[41]

This reminds me a lot of electronic circuitry. By the As Above: So Below rule, we can draw an analogy.

The Tree of Life is a Circuit Diagram.

But what's it a circuit diagram of?

Considering that the Bible is about soul and spirit and mind and morals, we might learn a lot by considering the Tree of Life to be a circuit diagram of the Mind of Man.

And indeed, Kabbalists talk about a concept called Adam Kadmon—a kind of abstract prototype for the first human, a celestial pattern to generate humanity, or the Architect's plans for building a human.

The Tree of Life pattern can be mapped

40. Liturgical poets call the Torah the Tree of Life.

41. There are a lot of different patterns for that energy flow that Qabalists discuss at tedious lengths.

onto a human body, and the circles along the central vertical line fall on the areas the Orientals call chakras (the psychic centers), the points in the aura where the soul is connected to the physical body.

Recall that I mentioned the origin of the dictum <u>As Above: So Below</u> is a text called *The Emerald Tablet of Hermes*, a Greek god. Well, that text bears an eerie resemblance to a Hebrew text called the *Sefir Yetzirah* which describes the generation of All Reality via the words of God.

The *Sefir Yetzirah* is thought to be the origin of the Tree of Life glyph. It supports the <u>As Above: So Below</u> principle without actually stating it quite so succinctly.

The trick to applying the Tree of Life glyph to real life situations is to understand that it's an archetypal pattern that can be recognized on the highest abstract planes of reasoning and on the lowest planes of perception. It is

Qabalists work with a glyph formed from the Tree of Life repeated four times.

the road map for traveling mentally up and down the levels of abstract thought. In other words, it's a master equation like the Unified Field Theory that theoretical physicists are still seeking in order to unite Einstein's equations.

The Tree of Life glyph represents the "smallest indivisible unit" of subjective Reality, but it's only an atom, not a molecule.

The Tarot structure is more extensive than the single Tree of Life glyph. There are four suits of ten numbered cards, so that there are four different cards on each of the numbered circles. The Tarot represents a whole molecule, or by the phoneme analogy, a whole word.

The Qabalists work with a glyph formed from the Tree of Life repeated four times, (corresponding to the four "Worlds" of the Qabalah). They chain the Tree of Life glyphs together, not end for end, but with the bottom circle of one attached at the center (or 6th) circle of the one below it so that they halfway overlay each other.

Then the Qabalists still talk about energy flowing down this pattern along various channels and moving from glyph to glyph at the points where they touch. Mathematically, this jump of energy from glyph to glyph would be akin to a translation/rotation into another dimension.

Now we have a glyph large enough to contain the whole Tarot deck.[42] It's a device commonly

42. Note that to lay out this pattern, you'd now have to duplicate the Major Arcana. Also note that each Major has several meanings listed in any book on the Major Arcana. And each Major is an ensemble of symbols. Each single Major Arcanum represents several different sorts of experiences which are nevertheless related to each other.

called "Jacob's Ladder" (see illustration below).

Yes, the reference is Biblical. It is the ladder in Jacob's vision of angels coming down from Heaven and returning.

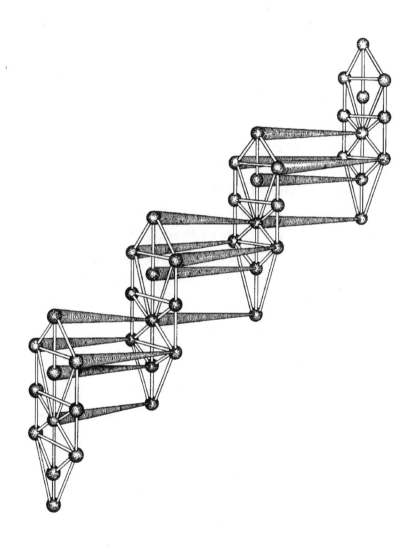

The Qabalists work with a glyph formed from the Tree of Life repeated four times, corresponding to the four "Worlds" of the Qabalah.

The conclusion is inescapable. The Tarot is intrinsically Biblical, not Hellenistic. Whatever oddball symbols you paint on the cards, as long as you maintain the structure of the deck, the Tarot is Biblical. It's the road map the soul must follow to Heaven. You can change the road sign language, insert false detours, distort the symbolism, or update it to speak in the modern vernacular as the older cards spoke in the vernacular of their day, but the Ladder still leads the mind through the subconscious to wherever God is.

So where is scientific "objective reality" in a circuit diagram of the human mind?

Remember the discussion of Free Will? We explored the idea that God created man in His own image. Of course, we don't know for sure what "image" means, but given the Tree of Life glyph we suspect what it might mean.

What if "image" means not physical form (since God hasn't revealed Himself via one) but a mental circuit diagram? What if the circuit diagram of the mind of man is the same as that of the mind of God, just smaller, carrying less voltage?

Then suppose that the Tree of Life glyph can be regarded as the circuit diagram of the mind of man *and so therefore* of the mind of God?

What *is* the mind of God?

One of the features usually drawn on the Tree of Life glyph is an arch over the topmost circle composed of three lines. Those lines represent levels of existence, non-existence, and eternity...or everything outside Creation.

Somewhere above and beyond Eternity is where God exists. Forget it. We can't conceive such a thing.

In our daily lives, we have all we can manage to deal with Creation itself. And so for our daily purposes, it's enough to consider All Creation as the crystallized thought of God, or perhaps a projection of the mind of God. Reality is the mind of God.[43]

Of course, it's not all of that mind. Forget it. There is such a thing as abstraction overload.

But the concept of reality as the mind of God does give us a handle on our essential problem in

The Tree of Life diagram is "holistic." Each part contains all other parts.

this chapter: Do the principles behind Tarot defy science? Or put another way, do you have to choose to be a scientist or a mystic, or can you be both without making yourself neurotic?

If the Tree of Life glyph is the circuit diagram of the human mind, it can be a powerful tool for mapping the subconscious and describing subjective reality. But it's also a diagram of the mind of God, which means it's a diagram of

43. That's why, when asked for His identity, God said, "I am that I am." That's no kind of a name even in Hebrew. He was saying that He is existence. That's what "to be" means, to exist.

All Reality, objective included, which means it can deal with both internal subjective reality, and the external, objective reality that science deals with.

What a daring concept! Maybe it's not true, but it's worth thinking about. Let's see where it leads.

Qabalists talk a lot about what they call Four Worlds, and I've described their glyph called Jacob's Ladder. But what *are* the Four Worlds?

Ah, we get into that and we'll be here a hundred years and still not have a way to learn about Tarot reading. Let's take a shortcut and just discuss the Four Worlds in terms of the Four Suits of the Tarot.

Decks differ in the symbols used to distinguish the suits. To me the symbols themselves don't matter as much as that they be easily distinguished from one another.

For this discussion, let's use the Waite Rider deck drawn by Pamela Coleman Smith under the direction of Arthur Edward Waite. This is arguably the most popular deck and the one I recommend to beginners because it is the least dangerous one I know of.

So the suits of this deck are called wands, cups, swords, and pentacles. Authorities differ on which suit to assign to which world, but for our purposes let's do it this way:

Wands corresponds to the World of Aziluth
Cups to Briah

Swords to Yetzirah

And Pentacles to Assiah.

That means that Wands cards represent the absolutely highest level of abstraction within the context under discussion. Regarding the Tree of Life as the mind of God—that would be so abstract that you'd go crazy thinking about it. Regarding the Tree as the mind of Man, it's easy...Wands represent Ideas.

The Ace of Wands represents the first in-rush of idea energy. Three bored kids, and one leaps up and yells, "I've got an idea! I know what we can do this afternoon!"

Cups represent the emotional reaction to the idea, the strength and energy that whooshes into existence because an Idea has finally occurred. It's the excitement generated by the vision of how much fun this game is going to be.

Swords represent actually doing the activity, running down to the creek to swim under the forbidden waterfall.

And Pentacles represent the physical result, the dead bodies floating in the creek.

Or alternatively, "I know how we can make a big profit off this one!" followed by the emotional euphoria that lasts through many gallons of midnight oil. Then comes Swords: sending out the advertising for the new store's grand opening sale. Counting the money is Pentacles.

Processes propagate down the Four Worlds of the Tree.

Note that the bottom world, Pentacles, is the

concretization of the process, the materialization of the results of the idea, emotion, and action.

Pentacles is a whole "World." It has an entire Tree of Life glyph that describes its internal structure.

One other point: the Tree of Life diagram is "holistic." Each part contains all other parts, each 10/22 unit contains the whole Jacob's Ladder.[44] The bottom World, Pentacles, contains all the above Worlds as well.

In many Tarot decks the Pentacle symbol is inscribed on a coin, so the suit is called Coins. In other words, the Fourth World of the Qabalah is money. Why?

Money symbolizes the result of idea, emotion, and action. Money is stored potential energy, like the charge in a battery. That energy originated not with man but with God. Thus, in the value system inherent in the Tarot, money is sacred, not the root of all evil.[45]

By one way of looking at it, Jacob's Ladder is a circuit through which Godshine flows from

---

44. Modern experiments seem to indicate the human brain stores information holistically, with a memory not stored in one cell but in many cells.

45. CAUTION: One of the oldest scams in the book is the gypsy fortuneteller who claims your money is cursed or tainted, that you must withdraw it and bring it to be blessed. Of course, during this process, the money and the gypsy disappear. By no theory of magick can currency be cursed or carry a taint. It is sacred. Your wealth cannot be the source of difficulty in your life. Your attitude toward it can. If you've got "an attitude," blessing your money won't help. Exploring your subconscious pain will help.

the mind of God through the mind of man and into objective reality. One possible manifestation of that Godshine is money symbolized by ten cards in the Suit of Pentacles, representing ten levels of abstraction. Because it is crystallized Godshine, money comes fettered with all sorts of moral restraints on how it may be handled and the dire consequences of mishandling it.[46]

But according to the scientific view of reality, money is just symbolic man-hours and the only morality applicable to handling it is codified in the laws of society.

No one can deny the efficacy of science, and nothing—not anything that anyone has ever been able to do—can produce scientific proof that God exists, that souls exist, or that spirits are real. Never mind that God manifests via the human spirit. Science has disproved so many of our cherished "common sense" notions that the lack of proof for the spiritual/magickal view of the universe is nigh onto condemnation of that view as superstitious drivel.[47]

Why can't science prove God exists?

The answer is simple if you use this Tree of

---

46. Such as not accepting money in exchange for the wisdom of the Tarot, but only for the time taken from earning a living.

47. I'm not discussing the Laws of Magick here because the discovery, definition, and exploration of those laws stopped in the Middle Ages. Only in the 1980s has there been a new beginning, practicing magicians studying the Laws of Magick with the tools of science and publishing professional journals. But it's a very small, unfunded, and fragmented effort to date. Someday, we may have Laws of Magick as well formulated as our current Laws of Science.

Life/Jacob's Ladder model of the universe.

Study of the processes referred to by the 256 components of Jacob's Ladder lead to the idea that one concrete meaning for Malkuth in Assiah is the space/time continuum.

Money is an abstraction derived from the space-time continuum. The space/time continuum is actually a more concrete notion than money. It is the floor under your feet, the roof over your head, the tables and chairs in your room. It is the Earth, the Sun, the Moon, all the stars, and the distance between them. It is everything our five senses perceive, everything that has length, breadth, and depth and exists through time.

Science, in all its glory, can only study Number 10 in Assiah. That tenth circle at the bottom of the Fourth World symbolizes all of what science calls the space/time continuum. Not all of existence, not all of reality, not all of the universe that God created in six days. Just the space/time continuum. The space/time continuum is the clockwork mechanism science has described it to be.

Inherent in that clockwork is all the rest of creation, and God's presence. But we've hardly scratched the surface of what there is to learn about that clockwork. While we're busy studying it, God is loath to disturb it lest we fail to see the "Below" clearly enough to discern the "Above" that is much like it. As we learn about momentum, we learn how to study the laws of karma. This is our playpen, and it's safe.

Outside Malkuth in Assiah is a region outside where time is defined, outside where space (distance; the three dimensions) is defined. This is the first, lowest level of what magick calls the astral plane and from there on up things get difficult to relate to.

Money is an abstraction of the space-time continuum.

With Jacob's Ladder, we're talking about a model of the universe that has 256 components of which all of science to this day has studied only two.[48] It's done a great job of studying those two, but it's only a tiny bit of the whole.

Looking at Jacob's Ladder this way, one no longer has difficulty with the apparently mutually exclusive views of science and religion. Most of what religion is about is in the 254/256ths of the universe that science hasn't studied yet. When we have a complete scientific understanding of Malkuth in Assiah, we will have a complete pattern "Below" which can then help us understand the unseen, unseeable, and unknow-

48. 62X4—we've left out the court cards because that's an 8-hour Master Class workshop in Tarot, but they do fit into this model very neatly. We've also ignored the Sefirah called Da'at because that's a Master Class in Qabalah.

able[49] dimensions "Above."

By the As Above: So Below principle, many methods of studying the sacred space/time continuum will be useful when we mount a systematic study of the rest. The Roger Bacon of magick hasn't published his books yet (I don't think). Very possibly, the Aristotle of magick hasn't even been born yet.

Clearly, if there's anything to this theory, the Roger Bacon, Aristotle and Pythagoras of magick will have to learn Tarot or something like it before they can contribute to the systematic formulation of the Laws of Magick and make those laws as efficacious as the Laws of Science.

Consider now, the kind of information the Tarot can reveal to a reader who can interpret it on such a level and if you have the capacity to receive it. The Tarot is to the circuits of the human mind what an oscilloscope is to an electronic circuit. It's a tool for troubleshooting the circuits of the mind, the spirit, and the soul to discover why a person is having problems manifesting the Godshine that always flows through his/her circuits.

Tarot does not defy science, but rather science is a special case of Tarot. Tarot is not devil worship or witchcraft, though people involved in both have used Tarot as they use inverted crosses and love potions to coerce another to

---

49. "Unknowable" in the sense that we must find words for the other methods of apprehension besides knowing.

their will.[50] They've used Bibles that way, too.

How a tool is used doesn't say a lot about the inherent nature of the tool. Looking very closely at the tool and what it does best can tell you more.

A close look at the Tarot reveals its sacred origin, even though Art Historians and researchers haven't found out who invented it or why. The moral philosophy innate in the cards is the Biblical philosophy[51] of which the Hellenistic is a special case applicable only to 2/256ths of what the Biblical philosophy addresses, while humans live their lives in the 256/256ths of the universe.

That's why no Biblical argument has ever disproved a Hellenistic premise. The Hellenists are right. They're just not talking about what we're talking about. Their only mistake is in thinking they're talking about the whole of reality. Our problems with Hellenism stem from trying to apply that philosophy where it doesn't apply—outside its domain of definition. It's like trying to solve a problem in atomic physics using only Newtonian Mechanics.

Science, then, can be profitably viewed as a

50. Note that real witchcraft as practiced by modern neo-pagans forbids practitioners to use any sort of power to dominate another person or even to command Nature to their will. Gaining power in order to force things to happen in a way that is to your advantage is Black Magick. People have used Tarot in that endeavor, too.

51. Which doesn't necessarily put it at odds with that of other sorts of religions. Most religions subscribe to certain basic precepts and all the systems of magickal training I've run into have similar behavioral strictures and principles.

branch of magick and the Tarot as a magickal tool which can handle science just fine. But its main application is in the realm of the human mind, soul, and spirit as we struggle on the journey back to God.

For that journey we first need to learn to drive, and then we need a good road map and somebody who can read the language on the road signs. For some seekers, under certain circumstances which only the seeker himself can judge, that road sign reader can be a Tarot reader.

VII

What Does a Tarot Reading Really Tell You? How Do You Tell Whether A Tarot Reader Is Skilled Enough And Wise Enough To Help You?

To prepare to discuss these questions, we've covered a lot of ground, using analogies from a dozen different fields. Most readers may have understood only half of what's presented here, and that's all right.

It isn't necessary to understand it all to apply it to the problem of understanding and reading Tarot and/or finding a good Tarot reader. (Though the following focuses on finding a Tarot reader for yourself, it also applies to anyone coming to *you* for a reading.)

Your main tool is your own personal ability to judge other people, to take the measure of a man or a woman. If you're good at that, you'll be good at finding a Tarot reader. And if not, you'd better take a friend with you.

Personally, I stay away from the gypsy-costumed hippies unless I know them personally and have seen them dress that way all the time, or know how well they read. At a psychic fair—the shopping mall type of event—the custom has grown up to dress the part and use theatrics.

If you go to someone's house for a reading you should find them dressed as they'd dress every day, which should be more or less the way you dress when busy around the house.

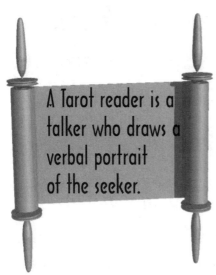

A Tarot reader is a talker who draws a verbal portrait of the seeker.

That's right, you want to find a Tarot reader who has a lot in common with you. Face it, people "Dress for Success," that is, they dress to advertise their position and philosophy of life, or to make you think what they want you to think about them...to manipulate you.

It helps to know your Tarot reader. Though strangers can give you better readings because they have the fewest preconceived notions about you, the better you know your reader the better you can judge their abilities.

One way to know a reader without their knowing you is to go to a psychic fair or some other gathering, convention, seminar, or workshop, and watch the reader read Tarot.

Now the idea of *kibitzing* while people discuss their personal problems in public may make some people squirm, and the idea of doing it yourself may be even worse.

The material you want to consult about is usually personal and private...such as whether to ask for a divorce, whether to quit school, whether to quit your job, whether to propose marriage, whether to break off an affair with a married person. You don't want it to get around that you're thinking such things.

In many cases, the problem the seeker is wrestling with will be so personal (Am I homosexual? If not, why am I impotent with my wife?) that they don't want to tell anyone, least of all a total stranger, and God forbid not in public.

Well, oddly enough, the reader doesn't have to know (and does better without knowing) what the topic is. A Tarot reading isn't a psychologist's consultation, (though many Tarot readers are psychologists, psychiatrists, or licensed pastoral counselors). Nor is Tarot a place to go to get answers or directions on what to do about your problem.

A Tarot reading wouldn't say whether you are homosexual or not. It would discuss why you have a problem with that concept. A reading is most useful when you are absolutely certain you know what your problem is, but nothing's working.

Under such circumstances, you're usually wrong about what the problem is. A Tarot reading can be useful in sowing the seeds of doubt, but it can be most effective when you already suspect you've been barking up the wrong tree.

A Tarot reading can also be effective when you are convinced your problem is unique so there's nowhere to turn for experienced advice.

Human problems don't come in Unique any more than human people come in Perfect. Since your problem isn't new or unique, if there are ten onlookers at a Tarot reading, nine of them have had that problem in one form or another.

The *forms* make our problems look unique. Tarot is for stripping away the manifested form of a problem to reveal the ultimate archetypal nature of the problem. Once the archetypal nature of the problem is known, the archetypal solutions can be applied, and the problem will begin to yield. Note *begin*; these are rarely one-step processes.

Since the reader deals in archetypes, each onlooker at a Tarot reading will recognize something they have wrestled with, without knowing what you're actually going through.

Tarot deals with patterns—not particular manifestations.

As a result, you can have a very personal conversation about truly intimate matters right out in public and have it be completely private. Nobody will guess what your problem actually is, but they'll sympathize from personal experience.

Tarot "debunkers" point to this phenomenon as proof that Tarot readers are all charlatans making up the usual fortuneteller's pitch.

Debunkers cite the fact that a Tarot reader can't tell you how the archetype has manifested in your life as proof that the Tarot reader is just handing you a line of bull and you're gullible enough to fall for it because you want to.

I'm not saying that doesn't happen a lot, especially at psychic fairs that aren't sponsored by recognized occult groups who screen their readers carefully. Charlatans and confidence men see people parting with large sums of money for a reading and figure that Tarot reading ought to be easy to fake. With clever theatrics, they can convince people to believe anything

Tarot deals with Patterns—not particular manifestations.

and "cross the palm with silver." Lots of silver. In fact, clever theatrics are more convincing to the non-reader than a real, honest reading. This has been true since Biblical times and is a very good, practical reason to "throw the bums out" of your town.

But after reading this book, you should see why a Tarot reading can't reveal anything individual about you, any more than an oscilloscope can read the serial number on a computer's case. As an oscilloscope, Tarot can only compare your current condition to your ideal condition and point to the problem.[52]

The Tarot reader doesn't want to know and doesn't need to know anything specific about you. When the reading is finished, you may want to talk about the particular manifestation your problem has in your life, but then you are consulting the reader on a different level from mere Tarot reading. That's okay, most Tarot readers know several other counseling techniques, but you should know this part of the transaction has nothing to do with Tarot reading *per se*.[53]

Tarot makes a good adjunct to psychological, spiritual, or psychic counseling for exactly this reason: discussion can shift back and forth

52. A good psychic can get information—very specific information about the seeker—by clairvoyant or precognitive flash. This does not come from the cards but as a side effect of learning Tarot. When focused via Tarot, psychic perceptions may be orders of magnitude clearer. If a complete stranger starts guessing specifics about you which are eerily true, you are dealing either with an accomplished psychic or a charlatan who has "cased" your life preparatory to pulling a confidence game on you. For this reason, legitimate psychics who read Tarot don't generally blurt out the specifics they happen to catch unless you've specified that you want a psychic consultation. If a Tarot reader is focused enough to help you, he/she can't help picking up peripheral data. A good psychic counselor reading Tarot will use all information to help you understand your position and take command of your own destiny, and a good Tarot reader will feel no personal need to impress you with how "real" or "brilliant" their psychic gifts are. A person who covets your admiration is not a good Tarot reader for you.

53. Note that the time spent drawing on a Tarot reader's counseling training should be paid for at the going rate in your community for psychological counseling. Spiritual counseling is generally available free through your religious organization. Learn to distinguish between psychological counseling and spiritual counseling as distinct from Tarot reading.

from the abstract patterns that connect us all to the particular manifestation in your life.

If you're looking for counseling above and beyond the Tarot, then look for someone with the appropriate counseling credentials who happens to read Tarot.

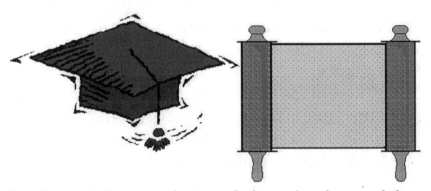

In order to practice any profession — whether you're a lawyer, a baker, a writer...or a Tarot reader — one must study first.

So how do you recognize words designed to counsel as opposed to the Tarot reading itself?

A counselor is basically a listener, an active listener who encourages the person to talk about problems and to listen to the words that come flying out in moments of emotional peak. Since Tarot reading needs raised emotions to be effective, any seeker who is getting a good reading is in a highly unstable emotional condition. It is easy to elicit such "blurted truths" from a person in that condition.

The skill of a Tarot reader lies in the gentle and subtle way he/she enters into an unspoken contract with the seeker governing how and when such material may be elicited, and then what may or may not be done with the material.

In a private group Tarot reading session, such as at a private party, there is the opportunity for a qualified Tarot reader to lead a group therapy session that can do as much or more good as a simple Tarot reading.[54]

Listen to a lot of Tarot readings done by different readers and learn to distinguish the moment that discussion switches from counseling to reading. A good Tarot reader allows the seeker to control that moment and the depth of the counseling discussion. Deeply personal matters can be reserved for a private counseling session at the Tarot reader's office. In truth, such matters can't be addressed properly in a fifteen minute reading at a psychic fair.

So what do you listen for that distinguishes Tarot reading from counseling?

By contrast to the counselor, who is a listener, a Tarot reader is a talker who draws a verbal portrait of the seeker. A Tarot reader is an artist who can draw such a personal portrait that the seeker both recognizes him/herself, and sees something they've never noticed before but can't deny. The Tarot reader also can place this

---

54. In fact, many students of Tarot regularly gather with other students of Tarot to engage in this kind of transaction aimed at personal growth. Tarot is a particularly effective focus for such sessions because it can reveal the patterns connecting a group, a set of problems these people all share and thus can help each other with.

portrait into an overall sketch of the seeker's position in life, a rendition which can reveal the deeper spirit just as an artist's brush can reveal the hidden truths of a person's character. All of this is done with words, just spoken words.

Occasionally, the good Tarot reader will do a "reality check" by asking the seeker short yes/no questions, such as "Am I right? Is this what was bothering you? Does this sound at all familiar? It looks to me like you were trying to focus on your marital problems, but this reading insists it's about money problems. Shall we discuss that or try another shuffle?"

Sometimes a reading picks up static in the room, or the seeker's other, unrelated problems because the seeker was distracted as the cards were cut, or sometimes the previous seeker's "vibrations" were still in the deck. A good Tarot reader will do one of several things: either switch to a different deck, reset the wards on the room,[55] sort the deck out into its original order and reshuffle, or talk the seeker into a narrower, more focused concentration.

---

55. Part of a Tarot reader's training is in the magickal act of warding or guarding the working space from outside noise or static. There are as many procedures for this as there are readers; however, it generally consists of nothing at all theatrical. Sometimes a reader will ask a seeker to sit quietly and meditate or pray for a few moments. Warding consists of nothing more elaborate than asking God's blessing as one might over a meal. Seekers who are well versed in spiritual practices may be invited to call on that training. A group may be led through a guided meditation. If you encounter someone who makes a big theatrical to-do about it, you know you're dealing with someone more concerned with impressing you than with accomplishing the warding task.

Once you've learned to distinguish Tarot reading from counseling, what do you listen for in a Tarot reader's words to discover whether they're any good at reading Tarot?

In previous chapters, we discussed the fortuneteller, and all the reasons to avoid them. It should be easy enough to spot a reader using the Tarot for fortune telling. They will keep saying things such as, "In March, watch out for people trying to swindle you." "There will prob-

The Tarot itself can not predict death.

ably be a lot of money available to you by summer. Spend it wisely, for there won't be any more for a long time." "You will have the opportunity for an extramarital affair. But there is danger down that path."

What can a diviner who is *not* trying to tell your fortune say on these topics?

"It seems that in the recent past, you have been in a passive mode of functioning, not paying sharp attention to your financial affairs. Is this true?"

"Oh, well. I've been very busy, you see, with this nagging problem—"

"Human nature being what it is, you might be inviting people to take advantage of you. The other day I noticed in the ephemeris that Neptune will be making a station right around your second house cusp the week of your birthday, so that could be a particularly challenging time in your material affairs—and that doesn't mean just money.[56] Time is a material resource, too, and has to be budgeted. The second house also represents values: what you think is more important than something else. Perhaps with a little work, you can clear up what's been distracting you and start sending the message that you're no one's mark."

Or, regarding impending wealth, "Recently, you've been working awfully hard but with no tangible rewards. If you choose to keep working at this pace and with such meticulous care, you should experience some degree of overt success from it eventually. But this reading indicates some problem with deriving satisfaction from that success. It seems you may have been considering dropping this line of development and restructuring your life toward different goals. Have you carefully considered what it is you really want out of life?"

Here the Tarot reader needs only a yes or no answer, and the next question would be to ask

56. Finding a good astrologer is very similar to finding a good Tarot reader. Astrology, likewise, cannot predict your future, but it can come up with a lot more specific information than a Tarot reading can. Furthermore, astrology can build a time-frame around what the Tarot reveals, for most of the Tarot exists outside the space-time continuum whereas astrology is specific to our particular corner of the space-time continuum. Often a Tarot reader will ask for your birthday, and your rising sign and moon sign if you know them as well, then synthesize this into the Tarot reading. The two disciplines are both requisites in many occult orders because they are complementary.

if the seeker wants to discuss his/her overall life goals in another shuffling of the cards. The Tarot will not answer questions with information, but instead it will discuss your motives for asking the question.

On the other hand, the counselor using the Tarot might continue to probe into the nature of what the seeker wants out of life, to get the seeker to verbalize a life's goal, and then go back to the Tarot for an evaluation of that verbalization. A person who is thirsty for well earned rewards may harbor some unacknowledged confusion about his/her goals: Is it really worth all this work? The Tarot is the ideal tool for discussing that, but it can't tell you when or whether you'll get rewards, just how you'd feel about it if you did get them...or didn't.

Our Biblical philosophy of life indicates that if we work hard and keep our noses clean, we'll get enough material rewards to achieve satisfaction. But in the Biblical philosophy, which is the Tarot's intrinsic philosophy that can't be altered by altering the symbols on the cards, the ultimate source of our living wage is God's own hand. Thus, we are not at the mercy of our employer's anger or distorted perceptions. If we have behaved according to all the commandments, then getting fired will do us no damage, especially if we get fired for upholding Biblical morality.

Quitting just to avoid hard work, however, can have dire negative consequences on our lives, as by Biblical standards we are enjoined to do our work "by the sweat of our brows." Thus, the Tarot reader is constrained not to dangle the promise of a big bonus in front of an employee in order to induce them to stick at a job which is wrong for them. Likewise, the Tarot reader must not use the promise of untold riches to lure an employee away from a difficult but minimally rewarding job which is right for them, but odious.

The Bible does not promise riches to the righteous, but only a living wage and sometimes not in money. You get what you really need, not what you want. Sometimes what your soul needs is hard work and poverty.

It isn't the Tarot reader's business to judge whether a particular job is right for a particular seeker. The Tarot reader's job is to help the seeker apply his/her free will to making a choice they can live with, even if it's wrong.

As you can see from the above, it takes a lot more words and a lot more tedious thought to read Tarot on a level which is not fortune telling. How can you see whether a Tarot reader has done that tedious thinking?

You can listen for the quick, easy sentences that are essentially judgmental. We've all been sensitized to how, without thinking, a person can pass judgment on another person's values. This is especially treacherous in a Tarot reading because the seeker wouldn't be there if he/she didn't have a problem, and thus be looking for criticism.

The Tarot itself has an innate value system. It will flash warning signals into a reading when the seeker's value system is at odds with that innate value system.

It gets very tempting to say, "Aha! I see what you're doing wrong!" Or, "This is what you should do."

Listen for words like *wrong, should, ought, mistake,* and *supposed to be.* They can reveal where the reader hasn't gone very deep into the value system of the cards.

The value system inherent in the cards is appropriate only to a model of the universe which includes the immortality of the soul and the concept that the soul is on a journey back to its maker—to which all roads lead...eventually. The value system inherent in the cards assumes that the soul is eternal and not in a hurry.

Therefore, it's not "wrong" to be wrong, to make mistakes, or to do something other than we should or ought. No person "should" or "ought" to do or be what another person is because no two people are alike. We could only be alike if we were all Perfect.

This life is no "emergency" in the evolution of the soul. If we screw up, okay, we're immortal, we'll just have another chance next time, if not in another human body, then in whatever form comes next. And the Tarot doesn't comment on that form any more specifically than the Bible does.

The Tarot deals with the journey of the

soul and with the eternity of the spirit, not with the complexities of this life. Or at least it deals with this life only as the life manifests what the soul has been up to lately.

Before you can understand what a good Tarot reader is saying—or ought to say—you must grasp that one salient fact about the Tarot. It deals mostly with the immortal soul.

Therefore, a Tarot reader would not and should not predict death for the seeker or someone around the seeker. If you hear a Tarot reader say that, that should trigger your alarms.[57] The Tarot itself cannot predict death. Not just because predicting the future is impossible, but because the death of a body isn't a very important event in the evolution of an immortal soul. Nothing *important* stops merely because a body dies.

That is the value system inherent in the Tarot. We are immortal, and we have free will. The results of our past choices don't stop with death, nor does our capacity to repent and change everything.

Thus, when at a crucial decision point (and both Tarot and Astrology are good for detecting the approach of these points), a seeker's death

57. Psychics can pick up data on past deaths of mortal bodies the soul has inhabited, and sometimes even see the death earned so far in this current mortal life. But every good psychic knows that if it's in the future, it can be changed...though human nature being what it is, change of that magnitude is unlikely. Nevertheless, it is possible, so good psychic counselors never predict death—just danger. But then, we're always in danger.

isn't a consideration, for we all "die" dozens of times in a long lifetime.

"Death" in magickal terms means "rebirth." It is the process of changing the way you think about and value things so drastically that you literally aren't the same person anymore.[58]

The soul going through a physical death experiences it as a rebirth. Tarot can't register a difference between physical and psychological death because there is no difference.[59]

The decision point that might be a death experience will not be regarded by the experienced Tarot reader as any sort of emergency where it's crucial that the seeker "do the right thing" and then "everything will come out fine."

If you are confronted with a reader who regards life as a series of challenges in which it is crucial that you "make the right choices" *so that* therefore, "everything will be all right," (i.e. that you don't suffer any pain) then you are confronted with an immature reader or a charlatan.

---

58. For example, the experience that Christians call being "Born Again" is one manifestation of what is represented by the Death card in the Tarot. It's not necessarily pleasant just before it happens, or while it's happening, but everyone who's gone through it regards it as worth the trouble.

59. We were evicted from the Garden of Eden so we wouldn't eat of the Tree of Life and not die. Traditionally, this is viewed as a curse. Suppose it's really a blessing. Consider Chapter One where we discussed karma and reincarnation. Suppose we couldn't die and start over when we'd outgrown a persona. Then we'd be trapped forever in an infantile state, forever unable to climb Jacob's Ladder because of it. The Tarot won't discuss dying as a problem, but it will discuss the fear of it in considerable detail.

That's not to say that such a reader might not be just right for you now.

But a reader should encourage the seeker to be unafraid of mistakes, to tackle their problems and their decisions boldly and with the style and grace inherent in their natures, and to be undismayed by the pain of sharp backlashes from their acts. Such a reader is someone who has plumbed the depths of the Tarot. The Tarot will discuss our attitudes toward pain, and ways of getting through it, but never methods of going around it.

There's one other subject many who become involved with the Tarot will talk about a lot. That topic is "psychic attack." Considering the number of *things* that inhabit a perfectly healthy subconscious, and considering the nature of the dissociated plexus,[60] it's not surprising that many who mess around with Tarot (which leads into the subconscious) start perceiving psychic attacks where there aren't any.

Don't be confused. There really is such a thing as a psychic attack. And there are trained sensitives who can perceive it and distinguish it from *things*.

If a Tarot reader tells you that you are under psychic attack, or under some kind of curse, how can you decide if he's bonkers? A charlatan? Or for real....

---

60. Remember that a dissociated plexus often manifests as something "out there" or someone else doing the things that are making the person miserable.

Well, just as in any other area of life when someone tells you that your enemies are acting to destroy you, you should ask "What enemies? Why?" And match up motive, method, and opportunity.

If you do have an enemy who has the knowledge and inclination, connections, or abilities, to mount a psychic attack, then a corroborating second opinion of the diagnosis would be in order. You would want a psychic consultant, preferably one who does not take money for it. Religious orders are the best place to find such an objective observer.

But it isn't necessary to establish the actuality of such an attack to determine if the Tarot reader is a charlatan. It's not so much the diagnosis that tells the tale but the prescription. What does this Tarot reader suggest you do about your situation?

If he/she tells you to spend a lot of money, even if there's no apparent way for a percentage to get back to the Tarot reader, contact your local bunco squad. Quick.

If, on the other hand, the Tarot reader admits ignorance about the prescriptions for psychic attack, and does not recommend a friend of his/hers to take care of it for you (for a hefty fee, of course), I'd take it seriously.

More than likely a Tarot reader experienced enough to read "psychic attack" from the cards is also likely to know the standard procedures for derailing such an attack. The standard measures cost almost nothing—candles, incense, the usual religious articles you already have around the house—and a little of your time on a daily basis.

The props are not nearly as important as your mind and emotions. I'd advise a Catholic to go to daily mass for a few weeks. I'd advise a Buddhist to cleanse and tend his household shrine. I'd advise a Jew to have the kashruth of his mezuzah checked and to cleanse and re-kosher his kitchen and tend to his daily prayers. I'd advise a witch to be sure to light ward candles in the quarters in their house when they're home and tend their threshold wards.

And anyone at all, I'd advise to adopt a regimen of prayer at the bedside before retiring. Psychic attack is most effective on the sleeping mind, which leaves the subconscious wide open. Filling your house, your office, and your life with the presence of the divine entity who sponsors you on the inner planes will take care of any psychic attack.

If you don't have the acquaintance of a divine entity, there are magickal exercises for sealing the aura and setting household wards which most Tarot readers can describe. These are "plain vanilla" exercises, compatible with most religions. They include visualizing a white light around yourself, visualizing yourself surrounded by a mirror which reflects back any ill wishes aimed at you and lets through all the beneficent ones, and breathing exercises to reduce stress (high stress leaves you psychically vulnerable as well as lowering your immune system's resistance) so you can concentrate and visualize more effectively. Concentration wards off psychic intrusion.[61]

Practicing these exercises on a regular basis usually leads a person to make the acquaintance of their divine sponsor.[62]

If the prospect of psychic attack is bothering you, I'd recommend a book titled *Psychic Self-Defense* by Dion Fortune. It's been reprinted many times, comes in hard- and softcover, and is usually available at any occult bookstore, and some big chain stores. Fortune provides a common-sense, no-nonsense approach.

For those unread in the occult, I'd recommend Dion Fortune's *Sane Occultism*, which is likewise widely available. These are not usually in the public library, so they'd cost some money, but it's well invested money (from which I get not a cent) if the topic worries you.

If an experienced Tarot reader warns of psychic bombardment, and you have reason to believe

---

61. Contrary to popular notions, concentration isn't about what you fill your mind with; it's about what you exclude from your thoughts. To think about something very hard isn't to concentrate. To concentrate is to not think about everything else. Concentration is a state of utter relaxation. Filling your mind with one single thing is a form of tension. Under tension, you are psychically vulnerable.

62. That's not necessarily a desirable result for everyone under all circumstances, but it isn't up to a Tarot reader to call that shot for you. It's your freewill choice.

someone who hates you has the ability and inclination to mount such an attack (it's black magick to do so, so even someone who hates you virulently might not have the inclination because mounting such an attack—even by hiring someone to do it— does more damage to the "mounter" than to the target) *and* if the Tarot reader's advice takes the above suggested forms, I would definitely take the matter seriously.

Once you have the staunchest wards you can manage in place, then watch the person you suspect. If guilty, then within short order, something will happen to them which shouldn't happen to a dog. If you feel appalled, and pitying, maybe a little relieved, then you've probably done the right thing and will suffer no further ill. But if this makes you feel triumphant, you've got a very bad problem.

If you experience a euphoric sense of triumph when you have vanquished an enemy, especially someone who deserves it, it reveals that you hated that enemy. Worse yet, since you succeeded, you've experienced what psychologists call positive reinforcement; you've been rewarded for hating your enemy. So you are going to feel tempted to go after the next person who claims you for an enemy and vanquish them so you can experience that peculiar euphoria again. It's addictive.

A good Tarot reader can identify the pattern of cards representing that addiction because they've seen it in themselves and got to be good Tarot readers by working on the problem. Face it. We all have it.

Jesus of Nazareth was a very good Jewish boy who learned from the Jewish mystics of his time that a mortal will get nowhere worth going by hating his/her enemies, by fighting them and defeating them, humiliating them, punishing them. "Vengeance is Mine, sayeth the Lord!"

It's a basic Magickal principle inherent in the Tarot and known in the orient as karma. If you hate, you tie yourself to the object of your emotions and take on some of the coloring of that object. If you hate your enemies, you're in bad, bad trouble.

That's not to say you "shouldn't" hate your enemies. You're perfectly free to hate your enemies if you really enjoy it all that much. But if a Tarot reader sees that hatred in a reading, he/she is obligated to explain to you just how it is causing you problems.

People will often say about hatred or any emotion, "I know I shouldn't feel this way, but I just can't help it." A Tarot reader will often be as helpless at this declaration as any counselor would be. The seeker is really asking for someone to change their emotional responses *for* them—that someone else can make them feel as they *should*.

In the value system of Tarot, there is no such thing as an emotion you "shouldn't" be feeling. In fact, you should feel exactly as you do feel, because that is who you are. You are, however, perfectly free to change who you are.

Over the old Greek mystery schools were written the words, KNOW THYSELF. The way to get to know yourself is to feel your feelings. In this high-stress society, we often don't have time to feel feelings: to cry, laugh, exult, and mourn. Emotions take time to build and time to discharge, and we often don't have time.

Our prevailing culture seems to put a premium on remaining "cool"—dispassionate, uninvolved. For example, witnesses at a congressional hearing are not considered credible if they shout and gesticulate. That's called "losing it" and sure evidence that the person's words are not to be trusted. Emotion is something not displayed in the board room, or the court room, and is best left for the bar and the bedroom.

With that kind of a cultural attitude toward emotion, it's small wonder that the average citizen can only say of their emotions, "I can't help it."

But the Tarot is a tool which is for changing your emotional responses to events and situations. It reads the circuit diagram for emotional responses. It describes in exhaustive detail the process of changing from one emotional state to another, and how to master those changes, rather than letting them master you.

Emotional responses, as well as compulsive behaviors, originate in the subconscious or the nonverbal part of the mind. Inappropriate emotional responses, ones that can't be "helped," originate with the *things* that live down there, the neurotic blocks that kept us as children from succumbing to intolerable emotional overloads.

The Tarot takes us on a journey into the realm where those *things* flourish. After a few years studying Tarot seriously and under guidance, the student does begin to notice how his/her emotional responses change. Things which used to trigger fury are now only mildly annoying without repression or "control."

But to get this to happen, one must commit several hours a day for a good number of years, and use the Tarot as only one of many tools. It won't happen if the objective is to learn the Tarot in order to show off.

And it won't happen just by going to a Tarot reader. Such transformation comes from study of the Tarot. However, regular consultation with a Tarot reader who is dedicated to transformation often does awaken similar ambition in the seeker. And by knowing just what to expect from a Tarot reading and a Tarot reader, you can apply this knowledge when you begin reading Tarot for others.

But what if you can't find someone who is that dedicated or working that hard? What if all you can find are bumbling beginners? Is it hopeless? Is there no way short of learning it yourself to get a good Tarot reading?

What Can You Do To Get (or Give)
A "Good" Tarot Reading?

From the foregoing discussion it is clear that very few readers have the time, the patience or the interest to delve into the depths of philosophy we've discussed. Most seekers neither need nor want a treatise on philosophy. So most Tarot readings are going to be reading somewhere in the middle depths of the Tarot—not superficial, as a fortuneteller would, but not the dangerous depths of the subconscious either.

So what is a seeker to do if every Tarot reading encountered is violating the guidelines in this book?

Fortunately, the quality of the Tarot reading—i.e. whether it is helpful to the seeker or not—doesn't depend solely on the skills and wisdom of the Tarot reader.

It does depend, as mentioned elsewhere, on

the Tarot reader's ability to attain and maintain an appropriate level of consciousness—a light trance.

In that state, the Tarot reader won't remember a single word of what he/she said. As mentioned before, no matter how public the reading is, it is still ultimately very private— even private from the reader. Often, in the right level of trance, the Tarot reader doesn't understand a word he/she is saying and will often ask, "Does that make any sense?"

Very, very often it makes perfect sense to the seeker.

How does this happen and why?

It happens because the seeker is the key operator in a Tarot reading. That's right, the seeker, not the reader.

As explained earlier, the Tarot can't tell you anything you don't already know, because nobody can ever be told something they don't already know—at least not in the area of knowledge discussed by the Tarot (i.e. emotions, values, morality, maturity of soul, health of spirit).

In this area of knowledge, telling is not a method of informing. Experience is the only way to learn. If you have no internalized experiential referent for an emotion, the words for it mean nothing to you. One cannot discuss God with someone who's never encountered God.

The Tarot can't tell you something you don't already know, but it can tell you what you do already know—which can be a revelation!

Very often, a mortal can't see what's right before his/her nose. Very often what you know better than you know your own name (e.g. it's not a good idea to hate your enemies) absolutely escapes you in the moment when you need it most (e.g. when you feel a euphoric surge of triumph at vanquishing an enemy, it means you harbored ill will toward him/her, enough ill will to get you in trouble, in fact the trouble you've got right now stems from that tendency to jump up and down on your enemy's chest).

In the heat of the moment, you don't recognize or identify what you're experiencing in terms of the overall principles of the universe that you accept without question.

The Tarot reader's job is to make that connection between the archetypal abstract and the concrete manifestation. The reading should identify last month's emotional reaction as an example of hating your enemy and connect it to this month when you found out that the enemy's replacement in the office is twice the bastard the old one was, is already on your case, and won't get out of your face. You don't deserve this. Why is it happening? Should you quit this job?

Since most schools of psychiatry are built on a universe view which excludes God, most psychiatrists can't help someone with a problem of this sort. Divine justice as well as divine humor escape them.

If your situation is one which people encounter only at a more advanced age than the

Tarot reader has reached, very often the divine justice and humor of it all will escape the Tarot reader too. But, given the unspoken contract between you and the Tarot reader, you may use that reader to obtain the self-portrait you need to laugh at yourself and thus come to the epiphany that will change you and your responses.

Now, how can you go about this without becoming an adept of an occult order or spending twenty years in a cave?

It's not easy, but it can be done even by a beginner.

The central trick is concentration, and the focus to concentrate on is your own emotions.

In other words, you have to psych yourself into it.

Firstly, long before you approach a reader, you have to set aside your Hellenistic view of the universe and wrap yourself firmly in the Biblical view.[63] Then you have to pray or meditate, bringing yourself as close as you possibly can to awareness of God.

Holding this frame of mind, you bring up the problem that you have to deal with, and meditate on it, then pray for help with it. It may also be worthwhile to write an extensive diary entry on the problem, describing it in detail, searching for the origins of it, and then rereading what you've written looking for areas where

63. If you can't deal with the Biblical view, you don't need a Tarot reading.

you're blaming it on someone or something external to yourself.

If you have free will, so does everyone else. Maybe what you're dealing with originates in someone else's will. But the bottom line is this: if it had no relevance to a problem within you, you wouldn't be dealing with it in any form. The problem within you might be a mirror image of the problem that's originated by someone else's free will.

So describe both problems as a series of questions, and don't hesitate to pose questions you have no answers to.

Once you've analyzed it, go back to praying over it, especially during the last hours before sleep. If you still don't have a clue when you waken, then there's a good chance a Tarot reading might help, but only if, while you're sitting over the cards, you can summon the peak emotional pitch the entire matter usually generates in you.

When we analyze intellectually, we turn our emotions aside, but Tarot reads emotions. What you take to your Tarot reader is the thing about which you keep saying, "Boy that makes me mad!" Or whatever brings tears to your eyes.

On your way there, in your mind, tell the whole sordid story to an invisible friend, vent your righteous indignation, let the tears roll.

Don't worry, Tarot readers won't downgrade your credibility because you've "lost it." We're used to this. We can't really get anywhere until or unless you lose it, because "it" whatever it is blocks emotional responses and fuzzes Tarot readings. So red-rimmed eyes are not going to go against you with a Tarot reader.

As you enter the room where the reading will occur, invoke your warding system—even lapsed Catholics might want to make the sign of the cross; others might want to light an incense stick; some might bring a Holy Bible with them and set it on the reading table; others might pick

A skilled reader can break through your emotional barriers (stone); tears will fall, bring tissues.

up reciting a mantra or an invocation. Whatever your key practice, be sure to execute that practice within the reading area, and then pray for assistance and ask a blessing on the reader. That's a vitally important part: asking a special blessing for the reader, and the constant protection of your deity.

Then sit down and dwell on the matter at hand.

The Tarot cards take a sort of snapshot of your aura at the moment that you (or the reader) cut the cards. Your aura is a constantly fluctuating nimbus of energy laced with complex structures analogous to circuitry but carrying emotion, not electricity. Your aura, which is visible to psychics, changes radically with your emotional state and intensity. In a dim problem area, we need a flash photo, and the flash is supplied by your emotional intensity.

You need to have that peak intense emotion at the moment you cut the cards, while your mind is wholly focused on the problem area. This sharpens a reading and makes it much easier to interpret, less ambiguous, with fewer spurious cross threads. Less experienced readers have a hard time sorting out the noise from the signal.

Most Tarot instruction books tell the reader to get the seeker to ask a question silently because formulating a question puts a person in the frame of mind to receive an answer. But since the Tarot can't answer questions, only discuss the motive for asking, that's not too helpful in clarifying a matter.

However, most people who don't practice meditation couldn't achieve a receptive mental state without asking.

As discussed above, that receptive state is a dangerous form of vulnerability. To open oneself that much before a Tarot reader, you have to trust that reader's values and morality if not skill with the Tarot.

One way to reduce that vulnerability and take command of the reading is to set aside the questions you've formulated and come to a decision in the matter, take a stance, be assertive toward the cards, not submissive. Then at the moment you let the emotional storm from concentrating on the matter come to a peak, hurl your decision into that storm wind. In that instant, cut the cards. Then you must induce the necessary receptive state to understand the cards' discussion of your motives for your choice.

One method to induce receptivity is meditation or a meditation mantra. Another would be to imagine yourself picking up the phone and saying, "Hello." Another would be to think, "What?" as if you hadn't quite caught what someone said. Or consider how unlikely it is that you know everything there is to know.

Remember the story of the Zen Master who pours tea for his student while talking of something else—and lets the cup overflow until the student protests in bewilderment. And then the

Master points out that the mind is like a cup, when it is filled with thought nothing further can enter. In order to learn, one must become empty.

Visualize that cup and it may induce a suitably receptive state. You don't need to be in trance, but if you ordinarily work in trance, then it is perfectly appropriate. You do need to achieve a state of active listening in which you can hear what is being said as opposed to what you'd like to hear. There are as many ways of achieving this as there are people who've done it.

You'll know you've achieved it when you don't notice the noise around you. When airplanes overhead don't disrupt your concentration. When a distantly ringing telephone doesn't distract you. When the slap of a newspaper landing on the porch doesn't register. In this state, your bladder won't tense up and make you feel that you have to urinate, your chronic cough will  subside for a few minutes, your general bodily discomforts fade. Most of us achieve such a state while watching an absorbing movie or reading a book or working a difficult math or computer problem or talking earnestly on the phone to a confidant.

Never has a scientific experiment proven that Tarot works.

What makes this exercise different is that you must achieve the receptive state right on the heels of an emotional storm of a variety guaranteed to block receptivity. It's quite a trick and takes a bit of practice.[64]

The quicker one can shift from storm to reception, and the longer and more steady the receptive state, the less of the work the Tarot reader has to do and the more the reader will exceed his/her own abilities.

This must sound like ridiculous hocus-pocus to some of you. But if you think about it within the context of this book's proposed mechanism for the Tarot, it makes sense.

Never has a scientific experiment proven that Tarot works. In order to conduct a scientific experiment, one must be in a skeptical frame of mind, intent on proving or disproving a theory, on settling an argument, on finding an answer. That state of mind is aggressive, not receptive.

You don't have to "believe" in Tarot to see it work for you. You do have to be utterly receptive. The skeptic is not receptive; he's evaluating and re-evaluating aggressively, searching for the objective truth of the matter. But Tarot operates entirely subjectively.

Science is founded on the principle that the state of mind of the experimenter doesn't have a bearing on the outcome of the experiment. The

---

64. It can be done. One of the most successful Tarot reading sessions I have ever done was at a resort hotel nightclub not twenty feet from the band, during a Star Trek convention where I was a guest speaker.

only thing that counts is what the experimenter does, not what he feels.

But if you are to experiment with Tarot, as a reader, a seeker or both, you must explore a model of reality in which the emotional state of the experimenter affects the outcome more than the manipulations performed, and the outcome is entirely subjective.

To get Tarot to work, either as a reader or as a seeker, you must accept that the quality of the reading, its success or failure, is a product of internal emotional states. The reading actually has much less to do with the Tarot reader, the deck used, or the place the reading occurs— though all of those things are important—than with the seeker's attitude.

In other words, for a Tarot reader to exceed his/her own limits, you must come to the Tarot with your attitude already adjusted into the value system of the Tarot. My personal idea of one of the Tarot's inherent values is that your destiny is a product of your moment to moment decisions and you have the free will to change everything at any time if you're willing to pay the price. The price, as I see it, is to accept responsibility for your own life and destiny and come to the Tarot seeking an understanding of your position, how you got into this mess, and what your options are for getting out of it. Not what option you "should" choose—but what options are still available.

Without that attitude of personal empowerment and personal responsibility, Tarot might still work for you. But a skilled reader should know how and when to drag a seeker through the process of assessing the available options—and the reader will have to do less reading and more psychological and/or spiritual counseling.

With that attitude of personal empowerment and responsibility, I have found that an encounter with Tarot may change your vision of the Universe, God, Humanity, and the relationship among them. That could be disconcerting if you didn't even know you had such a vision.

The more you know about your inner self, the more useful the Tarot can be to you. At the same time, Tarot is the most effective tool I have ever encountered for learning about that inner self, so even if you start with virtually no self-knowledge, a hundred percent increase at each encounter can quickly build a respectable amount of self-knowledge.

If you don't want to know about your inner self, you don't need a Tarot reading, and you most especially don't need to learn to read Tarot.

If you do commit yourself to the path of self-knowledge, the best place to start is by consulting Astrology and Tarot. As I've tried to establish here, one should choose consultants in these subjects with the same care one would lavish on the choice of a plastic surgeon to fix your nose, or a contractor to fix the foundation of your house.

But under no circumstances should you

ever "cross a palm with silver." Pay for consultation time, when you must, but never for the diviner's skills or wisdom. Whatever it is you're searching for, it isn't going to cost money. It's going to cost tears.

Mostly those tears are shed in grief over the years of your life wasted staunchly defending yourself from self-knowledge, being a helpless victim of bad luck, nasty employers, bad-tempered people, and irrational laws and rules. Some are shed in genuine remorse for the damage you've done to others while defending your tender inner self from the pain you've imagined to be too overwhelming to face. That neurotic pain, buried while you were less than about ten years old (when it really was too overwhelming to face), has to be disinterred and faced squarely in order to obtain self-knowledge.

That process is often referred to as clearing away neurotic blocks. For the sane, well-balanced personality, the Tarot is one (of many) of the tools effective in this endeavor, for even the sanest among us have such blocks.

Never Cross a Palm With Silver has covered some of the considerations common both to those who merely seek a Tarot reading, and those who are ready to embark on a path of learning Tarot.

There are many good beginner's books on Tarot. Ordinarily I recommend starting with the Waite-Rider deck and the instruction books by Eden Gray. When all of that has been digested and a number of other books, workshops, courses, and personal instruction sessions have brought you the ability to decipher a message in a Tarot layout, when you have tried reading for others and have discovered that you now have more questions than you started with—then you classify as what I call an "Intermediate" student of Tarot.

> If your miseries stem from having questions that don't have answers, I don't recommend the Tarot as a study.

There are so many good beginner's books on the market that I don't have to write another one. The next book in this six-volume series from Belfry Books will address such problems and puzzles that stop Intermediate students in their tracks and stall out progress. The Intermediate student quickly discovers there are few if any books on the market to help with this part of the learning curve.

Therefore, the second volume in the The Biblical Tarot series is: *The Magic of the Wands (The Not So Minor Arcana)*. It will focus entirely on the suit of Wands, exploring the Tarot in minute detail so that the student can independently determine what the value system buried behind the Tarot really is (as opposed to my personal opinion about it), where it came from, and how to apply that knowledge to derive fundamental, accurate, and personal meanings for the cards—instead of taking the word of someone who's written a book on the subject or drawn their own Tarot deck pictures, rearranging the symbols to suit themselves.

As I've said previously in this volume, the Minor Arcana are the most difficult to study and provide the main occupation of the Advanced Student. This series of books, The Biblical Tarot, is designed to bridge the gap publishers seem to have left between the plethora of excellent beginner's works on the market and the extremely advanced material, which is likewise excellent.

Each of the next four volumes of The Biblical Tarot will focus closely on a single suit in the Minor Arcana, and the final volume in the series will deal with the relatively "trivial" problem of the Major Arcana. (all of them in one slender volume). Taken together, these six volumes should be able to boost the dedicated Intermediate student into the advanced studies.

However, I do have one final caution for those considering learning to read Tarot. The most advanced level Tarot experts that I've ever run across have more questions than I do—and harder ones than I've asked in this book, too

If your miseries stem from having questions that don't have answers, I don't recommend the Tarot as a study.   On the other hand:

If you relish finding new questions because they shed light on previous questions, and for you discovering new questions changes everything in life in delightful ways;

If for you, Life Itself is the process of asking the next question and all the rest is waiting;

If for you "divination" means nothing more than discovering a new question, and that discovery pierces you with awe at the beauty of the world and causes you to "make a joyful noise before the Lord";

—then studying Tarot will probably do you a lot of good.

Glossary

adepthood An educational degree roughly equivalent to the Bachelor's.

alchemical Having to do with the science of Alchemy.

archetype A psychological pattern.

Aristotle Greek philosopher, 384 to 322 BC, a student of Plato.

Assiah One of the four worlds of the Qabalah usually referring to the world of matter.

Aziluth One of the four worlds of the Qabalah usually referring to the spiritual world.

Babylonian Exile Babylon was the capital of Mesopotamia on the Euphrates from about 2100

BC to which the captives from Judea were carried when the Babylonians invaded the country.

Bacon, Roger 1214-1294; English monk, he represented the necessity of a reformation in the sciences through different methods of studying the languages and nature.

Briah One of the four worlds of the Qabalah usually associated with the world of mental creation or emotion.

Caveat Emptor Latin for "Let The Buyer Beware."

Chakras A Sanskrit word usually meaning "wheel" and applied to a series of wheel-like vortices which exist in the surface of the Astral body of living creatures.

circuit diagram A blueprint for connecting the parts of an electronic or other energy handling device.

Da'at The eleventh Sephiroth on the Tree of Life and associated with knowledge.

diviner One who practices the art or act of fore-telling the future.

Einstein, Albert 1879-1955; The physicist who developed the Theory of Relativity.

The Emerald Tablet of Hermes The large pieces of emerald upon which Hermes Trismegistus (the Greek name for the Egyptian god Toth) is said to have carved the secrets of the universe.

ESP Extra Sensory Perception; general term for telepathy, clairvoyance, prescience.

glyph A pictograph or hieroglyph.

Hod The eighth Sephiroth on the Tree of Life usually associated with the scientific method of thinking.

holistic The theory that every part contributes to the whole. This is the theory behind holographic imagery.

Inquisition In the thirteenth century the Inquisition, an arm of the Catholic Church, set out to crush the arm of Christian Liberalism, the heretical movements foreshadowing Protestantism.

Kashruth The set of laws put forth in the Old Testament governing what may and may not be eaten.

knucklebones Ancient tool of divination; the bones of dead animals or humans.

magick In this book we will use "magic" to refer

to a stage magician's illusions, and "magick" to refer to the View of Reality which encompasses science, ESP, the eternal soul, and the Immanence of the Divine.

Major Arcana The 22 cards in the Tarot deck which do not appear in an ordinary playing deck.

Malkuth The tenth Sephiroth of the Tree of Life, usually associated with manifest reality.

making a station Astrology; an optical illusion that makes it seem that a planet in the sky has stopped.

Marrakech, Morocco A city in Morocco in Africa.

mezuzah A small case containing a paragraph from the Old Testament which commands that these words be inscribed on the doorpost of a house. It is usually nailed to the doorpost.

neopagan The Twentieth Century revival of certain religious practices devoted to various gods.

Netzach The eighth Sephiroth on the Tree of Life usually pertaining to the experience of beauty.

pentacle A five pointed star.

Pythagoras A sixth century BC Greek philosopher and mathematician.

Qabalist One who studies and/or practices the Qabalah.

Quarters The four compass directions, north, south, east, and west.

Rabbinic Of or pertaining to the judgments of authorities on Jewish religious law known as rabbis.

second house cusp A point in the Astrological birth chart which signifies things and ideas of personal value.

Sephiroth Any one of the circles on the Tree of Life Diagram.

sigil A signature or heraldic seal.

space/time continuum The three dimensions of space with time regarded as the fourth dimension.

Torah The first five books of the Old Testament (the five books of Moses).

The Tower A Tarot card from the Major Arcana, usually depicted as the Tower of Babel.

Unified Field Theory Albert Einstein's theory

that everything can be mathematically related to everything else. (This is an oversimplification.)

ward A protection, as in to "ward off danger."

Wicca A religion devoted to The Mother.

witch A practitioner of the nature religion that emphasizes herbal healing.

witchcraft The practice of the Wiccan religion, which has nothing to do with Devil worship. It is more akin to devotions to the Virgin Mary.

Yetzirah One of the four worlds of the Qabalah, usually pertaining to the world of formation or action.

yin/yang The Chinese philosophy of the combination of opposites within human physiology and psyche.

Background Reading

Albertson, Edward. *Understanding The Kabbalah*.
Los Angeles, 1973, Sherbourne Press, Inc.

Case, Dr. Paul Foster. *The Tarot, A Key to the Wisdom of the Ages*.
Richmond, VA. 1975, Macoy Publishing Company.

Case, Dr. Paul Foster. *Highlights Of Tarot*.
Los Angeles, 1970, Builders Of The Adytum.

Fortune, Dion. *Psychic Self-Defense*.
New York, 1976, Samuel Weiser Inc.

Fortune, Dion. *The Mystical Qabalah*.
London, 1974, Ernest Benn.

Fortune, Dion. *Sane Occulitism*.
London, 1969, The Aquarian Press.

Gray, Eden. *Mastering The Tarot: Basic Lessons In An Ancient, Mystic Art*.
New York, 1971, New American Library.

Kalisch, Rev., Dr. Isidor. *Sepher Yezirah*.
North Hollywood, 1973, Symbols and Signs.

Toffler, Alvin. *Future Shock*.
New York, 1971, Bantam Books.

About the Author

Gaining a degree in chemistry from the University of California at Berkeley with an eye to becoming a professional fiction writer, Jacqueline Lichtenberg spent the first twenty-two years of her life immersed in the scientific model of reality. But she became gradually more aware of the areas of life that science does not describe.

Unable to accept that the spiritual and scientific views of reality had to be mutually exclusive, she embarked on a twenty-five year odyssey in search of a model to encompass both views and resolve the apparent conflict.

In the course of publishing fourteen novels, she began studying Tarot, Astrology, comparative mythology, ceremonial magic, and related occult arts, as methods of improving her characterization and plotting while keeping abreast of advances in science such as the advent of Chaos Theory. Her public Tarot readings established her reputation for her unique synthesis of the scientific and mystical views.

For the last fifteen years, she has been conducting workshops to introduce beginning, intermediate and advanced students of the Tarot to the Qabalistic view of the deck, and has become a popular guest at occult gatherings and esoteric conventions.

She also uses the Tarot to teach the craft of writing. Many of her novels, under the byline Jacqueline Lichtenberg, incorporate karmic theories or exemplify astrological transits while drawing thematic material from the Tarot.

Though Tarot has become a large part of her daily life, this is the first nonfiction she's written on the subject. At the suggestion of her longtime friend, the editor, agent, and publisher, Sharon Jarvis, it incorporates the substance of two workshops honed from material developed over ten years of introductory seminars and given in 1991 in San Jose, California and Chicago.

Other Books
By Jacqueline Lichtenberg

SIME/GEN UNIVERSE:
House of Zeor
Unto Zeor, Forever
Mahogany Trinrose
Ren Sime

First Channel
Channel's Destiny
(by Jean Lorrah and Jacqueline Lichtenberg)

Zelerod's Doom
(by Jacqueline Lichtenberg and Jean Lorrah)

KREN UNIVERSE
(BOOK OF THE FIRST LIFEWAVE):
Molt Brother
City of a Million Legends

DUSHAU UNIVERSE:
The Dushau Trilogy:
Dushau
Farfetch
Outreach

OTHER:
Those of My Blood
Dreamspy

Boxmaster, written, unsold 1990
Limited Edition, April/May 1994 to be sold
Boxmaster's Disgrace, sequel written unsold
Limited Edition April/May 1994 to be sold
Boxmaster's Triumph, unwritten, unsold

Daniel R. Kerns titles:
Hero
Ace Science Fiction, pb. Oct. 1993

Border Dispute
Ace Science Fiction, pb. April 1994

NONFICTION BOOK:
Star Trek Lives!
(by Jacqueline Lichtenberg, Sondra Marshak,
and Joan Winston)

NONFICTION ARTICLES:
"Science Fiction Writers of America and the
Nebula Award" in
*Dictionary of Literary Biography Vol.8: Twenti-
eth-Century American Science Fiction Writers,
Part 2: M-Z*
Mathew J. Bruccoli, ed.,
Gale Research Company, 1981.

"Proposal for a New Genre," in *Midnight Zoo*
Jon L. Herron, ed., Oct./Nov. 1991

"Recommended Books," monthly column in
The Monthly Aspectarian,
P.O.Box 1342, Morton Grove, IL 60053.
March '93 to present.

"Millennium Prophecies," contributing editor.
St. Martin's Press.

SHORT STORIES:
"Operation High Time"
Worlds Of If Magazine, January, 1969.

"The Channel's Exemption"
Galileo Magazine, #4, July, 1977.

"Recompense," Galileo, #2, 1977.

"The Vanillamint Tapestry"
Alice Laurance, ed. *Cassandra Rising*.
Doubleday, 1978.

"The Answer"
by Jacqueline Lichtenberg and Jean Lorrah.
Marion Zimmer Bradley, ed., *The Keeper's
Price, and Other Stories*. DAW, 1980.

"Science is Magic Spelled Backwards"
Susan Shwartz, ed.,
Hecate's Cauldron DAW, 1982.

"Event at Holiday Rock".
Isaac Asimov, and Alice Laurance, eds.,
Speculations.
Houghton-Mifflin, 1982.

"Through the Moon Gate"
Andre Norton, ed.,
Tales of the Witchworld #2, hardcover edition,
Tor, May 1988.

"False Prophecy"
In Rachel Pollack, and Caitlin Matthews, eds.,
Tarot Tales, Century Legend, London, 1989.

"Aventura"
Marion Zimmer Bradley, ed.
Marion Zimmer Bradley's Fantasy Magazine #6,
1989.

"Mother's Curse"
In *Midnight Zoo*, Jon L. Herron, ed.,
544 Ygnacio Valley Rd., #A273,
Walnut Creek, CA 94596,
annual anthology, Jan. 1992

"Vampire's Fast".
Serialized in *Galaxy Magazine*,
E. J. Gold, ed., Premier issue, Vol. 1, Issue 1,
Jan/Feb., and March/April 1994.

From Jacqueline's Kitchen Table

The *Biblical Tarot* series explores what I call "Lichtenberg Originals": ideas, theories, postulates, attitudes, analyses...that I didn't get from anywhere. I made them up from my own personal understanding, gained by long hard practice and daily living. Very often I later discover that someone else thought of it first—like maybe a few thousand years ago. I find those little discoveries somewhat reassuring.

Yet there are a number of ideas here that I've never found in any book. I've explained most of them to rooms full of people at various lectures, classes, and workshops I've conducted. Many of these folk are "advanced" students of Tarot who'd been working at it for over ten years. And they couldn't recall hearing or reading these ideas anywhere else either.

Some years ago, people started suggesting that I should write them all down in a book. After all, that's what I do for a living...write books. It ought to be easy for me to just jot down what I'd said to them and make a book.

But I resisted for years. I write novels, fiction, science fiction, fantasy—not nonfiction. Of course, I had been the primary author of *Star Trek Lives!*—and though that's nonfiction, and has been used as a textbook, it's journalism, not mystical instruction.

Then it occurred to me that there weren't any books to

bridge the gap between the excellent volumes on the Major Arcana and Dion Fortune's masterwork, *The Mystical Qabalah*, which is about the Minor Arcana (a much more difficult and deeply mystical subject than the Major Arcana).

And I realized that folks were asking me to write such a work. They kept telling me that they understood while I was explaining the Minor Arcana, but a few hours later that understanding had evaporated to the point where they couldn't explain it to someone else. They wanted a book to take home with them, something to use to share their new insights with others. I thought about it, and began collecting my lectures and notes into this series of volumes, calling the project, *The Not So Minor Arcana*. And I fumbled and fumbled for years trying to find a point of entry into this material to make it accessible to someone who hadn't been through many of my workshops.

I started with techniques of writing from my original training in nonfiction writing from college papers. My university education is in the physical sciences, Chemistry, Physics, Math. I abandoned that career in the mid-sixties to raise children and write science fiction—for what Dion Fortune terms, "The Path of the Hearthfire." (Chemistry is easier!)

And I couldn't write the book these people had asked for. The style of writing didn't fit the material. The words wouldn't come together to make any sense at all. And then, in the early 1990s, I did a workshop at a World Science Fiction Convention, speaking to a room overflowing—full of not just science fiction fans, but people who had read my own novels and/or attended a number of my other Tarot workshops.

We had a language of discourse in common. They knew who Jacqueline Lichtenberg was and listened with that in mind...and understood. Out of that experience came Volume One of The Biblical Tarot, *Never Cross a Palm With Silver*. After years of struggling, I just sat down at the computer and wrote it—almost exactly as I'd said it to that group. Almost exactly as I've said it many times to groups gathered about my kitchen table.

So I am convinced that nothing I can write in these volumes will make sense to any reader until they have at least some idea of who I am, relatively speaking. Relative to yourself, whom I don't know!

So bits and pieces of me, personally, will be sprinkled here and there throughout these volumes. They will be, in many ways, just the sort of discussion that flows around my kitchen table over dinner. This will displease folks trained in modern Academe. In fact, it will make them look askance at these volumes and totally disqualify this writing from serious consideration by scholars. That is, of course, why other books on Tarot avoid allowing the author's personality to intrude on the work. If they did, they wouldn't be taken seriously because they'd be violating the rules of good scholarship.

I don't mind violating those rules. I'm not and never will be any sort of scholar, especially not of the Occult. I am a practitioner, a "down-and-dirty empiricist" with an imagination that works overtime creating new theories. I'm a theoretical philosopher.

So I'm going to tell you some of those theories (some of which contradict each other) and I'm going to reveal the steps in my reasoning that lead to those theories. If you can grasp my reasoning and follow my logic, you will finish these volumes and go off to create your own personal theories and practices—totally different from, and largely contradictory to, mine.

Let me put my approach in context for you.

This series of books on the Tarot has the overall title of *The Biblical Tarot* because it is based on (but not strictly derived from) the Qabalah. Let me remind you of the connection between Tarot and Qabalah. The Tarot deck itself, the number of cards and the sub-categories they are divided into, cause the Tarot Deck to look just exactly like the Qabalistic diagram known as the Tree of Life cut into small pieces.

If you lay those pieces out, they fit onto the Tree of Life diagram. "Tree of Life" is another term for the Torah, the First Five Books of Moses, the Pentateuch. Tarot, Qabalah, Tree of Life, and Bible are all words that refer to exactly the same thing. So the description "Biblical Tarot" is an oxymoron, or possibly an in-joke shared by the guests at my kitchen table. And we all invite you to enjoy the joke with us.

Now, there's one more important thing to understand here.

What I mean by "Qabalah" may be somewhat different from what others mean by the word. Therefore, you can't learn any Qabalah from this series of volumes on Tarot. But if you learn Tarot from these volumes, you may be able to apply that insight to unravel some of the secrets of Qabalah—if you can find a teacher willing to take you on.

Men who are deeply steeped in the teachings of the living tradition of Qabalah carried by an unbroken chain of Rabbis down the centuries have asked me, seriously, "Well, which school of thought do you belong to? What are you teaching these students of yours?" And they list the great and contradictory lines of development that have come down through the ages. When I answer just as seriously, "None of the above," it really puts them off. The natural inclination is to ask the same question again, phrased differently, as if I hadn't understood the question.

After the third time, I usually try to explain that I don't bother to deal with these distinctive differences because they don't actually matter to students exploring the Tarot from a beginner or intermediate perspective. The concepts I'm dealing with predate the split into schools of thought. Besides, I'm not a scholar, and being female, have not been admitted to that higher study.

So when I use the term "Qabalah" it does not refer to the inner mysteries of these secret schools of mysticism guarded and transmitted by our Great Sages, may their memories be blessed throughout all the ages to come.

N or does the term "Qabalah" in my hands refer to the various schools of pagan and neo-pagan mysticism that have spawned huge numbers of books in recent decades, many as outgrowths of Dion Fortune's work, and/or the Order of the Golden Dawn.

Then what am I talking about when I discuss "The Biblical Tarot"?

Qabalah (spelled variously because it's transliterated from the Hebrew letters by various linguists) means basically "Received." And what was "received" was the Torah, the First Five Books of Moses, a.k.a. The Pentateuch.

Torah means "teaching"—not writing, not saying, TEACHING. It is what was taught.

Now, everyone old enough to be studying Tarot at all knows that it's impossible to communicate with someone so much younger that they haven't got the experiential referents to go with the words. Experience is the only real teacher. Just try to explain to an eight-year-old boy what's so fascinating about a girl.

In the study of Torah, the word "teaching" is never used to describe the transaction that occurs when a group sits around a table and reads the text of the Torah along with the commentaries on it by the Great Rabbis. The process—regardless of how many other Great Rabbis are sitting around that table (usually a dining room table)—is referred to as "learning together." Nobody can "teach" Torah. It can only be learned and then only at great and persistent effort. It's not just memorizing, it's living, feeling, growing, being, doing, practicing, and it's not done just around the table. It's lived twenty-four hours a day.

F or those who have never watched this process going on around them in their own houses on a daily basis, I recommend reading the novels of Chaim Potok to grok the images if not the content. Juxtapose that reading project with the novels of Faye Kellerman about Rina Lazarus and

Peter Decker. Both sets of novels should be available through your local library.

That's a good long reading list, but if you're serious about learning Tarot, it won't seem overwhelming. Besides, they're all really good books—fun reading—like washing down these volumes of "death by chocolate" with some nice fresh cold milk. Remember that! These novels are confections, not nourishment. And you only get dessert after you finish your peas.

When you get done with those, and perhaps a short excursion into some of the more scholarly works on Qabalah, preferably the original sources such as *The Sefer Yetzirah* and *Bahir*, and *The Zohar*, you'll note something really odd.

Yes, admittedly, all of these works predate the popularization of "The Scientific Method." However, many do have something of the flavor of the teaching methods of the Ancient Greeks. They all consist of almost nothing but a disorderly—dare I say illogical?—jumble of personal quotations of Great Sages. At most, these pronouncements are surrounded by a few paragraphs of contexting, to indicate where the discussion took place, and what the subject of the discussion was before and after the Pronouncement.

And the most important thing about the Pronouncement is assumed to be the personality, daily habits, attitudes, and emotional responses of the Pronouncer—not the Pronouncement itself.

This is what we're talking about when we refer to a Received Text. The text itself is nothing more than class notes, an abstract, an outline. The meaning of those notes lies in the personality of the giver filtered through the personality of the note-taker, and those notes are just a means of investigating the giver's understanding of Reality.

And so it is with the Torah. The Torah was Received by Moses on Mount Sinai but the meaning of it was given to him by experiential referent, contexting into the whole and entire Personality of the Giver. Moses left us his notes, graven in stone, and an explanation of what those notes meant which was left as verbal instruction. And that verbal instruction wasn't classroom instruction. It was instruction transmitted by daily living, side by side, shoulder to shoulder, emotion to emotion.

That experiential referent that was given to Moses is called today Qabalah. And down through the ages, each generation of Rabbis that has Received it has explained it to the next generation as best they can. That accretion of explanations is what the scholars call Qabalah and it consists of these notebooks written by students who followed the Great Rabbis around and took careful notes.

But if you read any of these notebooks, you'll see that they consist of long and intense discussions, arguments actually, carried on in somewhat informal surroundings and circumstances such as walking in the garden, traveling down a road — or sitting at table.

And since none of this was written down until long after the fact, much of it is memories of what was said, or reports of what someone said a Great Rabbi said. You all know how accurately a message is transmitted in the game of "telephone." You all know how accurately people report to other people what you said in an emotional exchange.

Now, let's compare this with the teaching methods in other mystic traditions. The gurus and sages and avatars all around the world have "taught" or transmitted their wisdom, message, or insight, not by classroom instruction, using textbooks devoid of all the personality context of the author, but by sitting over tea with their students, by taking the student into their home, their life, and becoming part of the student's life.

It's all done with the rubbing of one personality against another, the intertwining of emotional realities, the interpenetrating of points of view. If the message you have to transmit is made out of subjective emotional experience, then the information of most value to your recipients is your personality, your feelings, your point of view, and your opinions. All those things are forbidden intrusions in "scholarship." Therefore "scholarship" isn't an appropriate vehicle for the transmission of Tarot. That's why I couldn't get these books written down when I first tried.

W hy? Because Tarot is about the subjective world, about internal experience, about your most private Identity. *The Biblical Tarot* allows you to look through my eyes and see the Universe that I see. Then look out of your own eyes, and study what you see. Analyze, contrast, and compare until you can find how these two visions of reality can both be mapped onto the Tree of Life. When you've got them both almost fitted onto the Tree of Life, and you can see how these two vastly contradictory subjective visions are both equally valid expressions of the underlying objective reality, then you can find the mistakes you and I are both making and set about improving your karma.

And in the process, you may be able to help some other people see your life through your eyes, and keep this process going.

So welcome to my kitchen table. And be warned. To follow the ebb and flow of the cross-chatter, to keep up with the offhand allusions, and to become part of the experiential referents, the deep and broad-flowing context, you will probably have to read more than just the books in this series. And a good deal of your time will be spent in dusty-musty used bookstores or on the Web searching out the material you need to read.

I t should be very easy to find out all you need to know about me by reading what I've written elsewhere. There are a couple dozen books and stories—science fiction, fantasy, Star Trek. And there are more than fifty essays that I've done on the occult sciences and the Initiatory Path of the Magician in the form of a review column of science fiction and fantasy, published by the New

Age magazine, *The Monthly Aspectarian*, and posted on the Web at http://www.lightworks.com

In addition, stories, novels, essays, illustrations and background material can be found at various websites, many done by fans of my Sime~Gen universe. You should be able to find some current URLs of these sites by searching on Sime~Gen and/or Jacqueline Lichtenberg, Zeor, Occult, sf, or related keywords. And that search should also bring you to a bibliography and aid in tracking down all these works in their most current printings/postings or publications.

One of the reasons for this extensive Afterword is a pet peeve. I have noticed one serious lack in all other books I've run across about the Tarot. That lack became more and more annoying as I progressed in this study. It is the sense of "who" the author of the book really is. The biography on the back doesn't help much because it's a piece of commercial writing designed to sell the book, not to reveal the totality of a personality. It's not there to "characterize" but rather to "credential."

The study of Tarot is the study of the subjective aspects of Reality, as "Science" is the study of the objective aspects of Reality. Yet most books about Tarot make "pronouncements." They say, "This means that" and "if this, say that" as if it were a cut and dried formula. Meanwhile, there is no information on the pronouncer by which to judge the applicability (not validity; applicability) of the particular pronouncement.

So, my intention in The Biblical Tarot series is to give you something of a feel for my "take" on the Tarot, the way I look at it, what I understand it to be, my personal theory of how it works and why it works. When you have reached the final volume, you will understand the mechanism behind subjectivity—the science of Tarot.

Excerpts from "The Magic Of the Wands"

A special sneak preview of the second volume in the Biblical Tarot series.

The following material is condensed from the Introduction and first chapter.

The Ace of Wands and God

This series of books is called *The Biblical Tarot* but it's not about God.

We are going to study the structure of the Universe that He created in microscopic and macroscopic views, and some of you may make inferences about God from what we see through the lens of the Tarot. But these books will have very little relevance to any particular theological position.

In this book, *The Magic of the Wands*, we're going to study the Tree of Life diagram. A Tree of Life diagram is an array of circles with three arcs above. The Ace of Wands is represented by the top circle on this Tree of Life diagram and the three arcs above that top circle are called, in Qabalistic parlance, Veils of Negativity.

Please don't be overly impressed with the jargon. It only means that nobody knows anything about them. Haven't you noticed that when scholars really know nothing whatever about a subject, they use words that don't mean anything?

Since this isn't a scholarly work, I can tell you that those three arcs are also called, *"Ain," "Ain Sof,"* and *"Ain Sof Or."* That's roughly transliterated from the Hebrew and it means: "There isn't," "There is no end," and "There is no end of light."

But what it really represents is the "place" or "realm" where God abides, outside existence, outside Creation which He hath created, beyond the outside of whatever we're inside of.

It doesn't seem reasonable to me to investigate what's on the outside of "this" before having glanced around to discover what "this" is, where its edges are and how the inside works. So when I first picked up a Tarot deck to find out what this thing called Tarot really is (as opposed to what all the books I had read said it was) and I began investigating my first Tarot deck, my first and most urgent question was, "Is the philosophy built into this thing in harmony with my own inner, spiritual life?"

If I had found that the people who created this thing called Tarot had woven values into it that I found abhorrent, I'd have tossed it in the trash. I have better things to do with my life than mess with stuff that is morally questionable.

It took me a long time to map the value structure inherent in the Tarot because all the instruction books start at the wrong end, and most of the writers aren't interested in passing judgment on the value structure woven behind the Tarot. Most writers of instruction books on the Tarot do it to make money off the readers' assumption that the Tarot can awaken psychic talent and allow ordinary people to foretell their own fates and future events in their lives.

Those of you who have read the first volume in *The Biblical Tarot, Never Cross a Palm With Silver*, know that one of my first discoveries is that the Tarot cannot be used for foretelling the future. This was one of my most early and most reassuring discoveries about this tool, but it took years to formulate, test, reformulate, and verify this hypothesis until I find it a firmly reliable theory upon which all the rest of my understanding of Tarot rests.

So, if the Tarot can't help you foretell your future or become a psychic in twelve easy lessons, why bother to study it? Why spend the next twenty years of your life toiling up a vertical learning curve, struggling to master this incredibly complex tool? If it's not for foretelling the future, then what is the Tarot *for*? And how could all these people who use it and write about it have missed that important point?

To answer that, let's go back to the Tree of Life diagram. The first card of the Minor Arcana is the Ace of Wands—that's the highest point on the Tree of Life diagram that has a Tarot card related to it. And it's nowhere near those three arcs, *Ain, Ain Sof,* and *Ain Sof Or*.

So God, and all the various notions of Who He Is and What He Wants Us To Do are outside the subject matter of the Tarot in any direct way.

The Tarot is a piece of machinery that "models" Creation. It can be used by atheists, agnostics, priests, ministers, psychiatric workers, psychics, or the psi-blind. In a vast and broad study of comparative religion, I haven't come upon a system that can't be mapped onto the Tree of Life, nor have I found a system that is precluded by the philosophy behind the Tarot.

From teaching Tarot, I have learned that if you perceive the Universe as having been Created by God, then everything you learn through the Tarot will reveal something about that Divine Personality just as an artist's work reveals something about the artist. If you perceive the Universe as a piece of mechanical machinery, then everything you learn through the Tarot will reveal something about that machine.

How can one tool, however complex, do two such contradictory and mutually exclusive things?

The answer to that comes back to the question, "What is the Tarot for?"

My personal answer to that question—after decades of skeptical investigation—is that the Tarot is for making connections and revealing the patterns. The Tarot is a tool for turning the circuit-board of the Universe over so you can see the soldering on the other side. Or put another way, it's a "collating rack." In this day of fancy copying machines, some of you may never have seen a collating rack. It's an upright, open cabinet with lots of little shelves. If you want to make 50 copies of a 20-page booklet, you put 50 copies of each page into each of 20 shelves. Then you take one page from each shelf in turn and stable the bundle together. And do it over 50 times.

That's what the Tarot is: a device for organizing the components of your knowledge so you can rearrange them into something else and learn something new. The rack itself doesn't contain the value or meaning. It's what you put into it and how you reorganize those pieces that causes meaningful results. The rack just makes the chore easier and more accurate. The rack works because it has the right number of shelves and they're the right height to contain the amount of pages you have to shuffle.

Likewise, the Tarot is a tool for doing a job. If you don't have that job to do, then you don't need this tool.

So, before the Tarot can be a tool worth years of hard studying, you have to know a little bit about a lot of things, and a lot about quite a few more things. You have to have lived long enough to begin wondering how all these different contradictory things you know can be simultaneously true. You have to be old enough to be worried about finding a coherent pattern behind all the different things you've learned, and old enough to be ready to be your own "authority" rather than believing what you've been taught.

The Ace of Wands
"Aha! NOW I get it!!!"

That burst of bright energy that lances through the mind-fog at the foot of the Steep Learning Curve is (for me, not for everyone) symbolized by the Ace of Wands.

I am assuming that most people reading this book are thrashing about in just such a fog where the Tarot, the Occult, and Mysticism in general are concerned. The first thing that most people do when they want to learn to read Tarot is to go buy a Tarot deck and an instruction book, spread this whole mess out on the kitchen table, and set to it as if doing homework for a course. I did that.

Because I had been given a really good clue about where to start, my entry into the fog was fairly smooth...but my first question took about ten years to answer. My question had come to me through a mentor giving me a book by Dion Fortune titled *The Mystical Qabalah*.

Dion Fortune's book is sprinkled with cursory hints about the connections between Qabalah and the Minor Arcana and doesn't touch on the Majors in any informative way. Each of ten chapters focuses closely on the inherent meaning and related symbolisms (correspondences) between the Sephiroth on the Tree of Life diagram. The relationship to a Tarot card is a cursory footnote. The book assumes you know all about the cards.

The fog closes in because all the available sourcebooks are commercial properties marketed to make money. And as far as I know at this writing, they all sell you on the idea that you can read this or that book and "unlock the secrets of this ancient, mystic art," gain mysterious power, predict the future, tell fortunes, reveal your past lives, find solutions to your personal dilemmas, and become a popular guest at parties.

There is a fallacy behind this sales pitch and the fallacy is simple. "Because the Tarot has been used for centuries to tell fortunes—*therefore* the Tarot must be able to tell fortunes." It must have been designed for fortune telling, it must be that if you can just learn the "secrets" of the Tarot, then you'll know the future. It is also "sold" that being a "good" Tarot Reader means being accurate about foretelling the future. And "scientific" type people point to the incontrovertible fact that Readers are most often wrong about the future as "proof" that the Tarot is garbage, nonsense, superstitious drivel, or charlatanism.

New students of Tarot, especially the young, almost invariably get caught in a vortex of anxiety and even nightmare terror when they "see" in the cards a horrible misfortune bearing down on them. In the grip of this paroxysm of Terror, they lose sight of the value of Faith in God and start thrashing about and very often end up in dire psychological difficulties.

Seeing this happen to young people convinces the Faithful that it must be the Tarot itself that is a tool of the Devil. Rarely do the Faithful ever read the Tarot instruction books that hint at a connection between Tarot and Qabalah and then go check out instruction on Qabalah and learn that you must be over 40 and married to begin to study Qabalah! And there are good reasons for that requirement.

Every last one of these reactions to discovery of Tarot is the result of believing what commercial interests use to sell lots of Tarot decks and books. It's an assumption buried deeply behind every cover quote, Tarot Card Box illustration, behind every one of Eden Grey's cookbook interpretations of the cards, and every marketing ploy, including Tarot readers on television talk shows or with 900-number advertising. Because the Tarot is being and has been used to foretell the future, *therefore* it must be a tool designed to foretell the future.

This is also one of the reasons why some people believe the Tarot might not in fact be the Tool of the Devil. But this is an assumption on just that level where challenges are most apt to be shattering. Giving up that assumption could be life-shattering, but not necessarily faith-shattering because the Tarot itself is built on the foundation assumptions behind faith.

The Ace of Wands is a case in point. Like every other Tarot card, the Ace of Wands has its origin in a Biblical passage—and takes its meaning from that passage. And it has nothing whatever to do with the Future. It has to do with the process of the Present.

I'm going to use easily accessible English translations to explain how I see this, but I want you to keep in mind here and throughout this book and every volume in this series that not only the original writers but also the translators and scholars in between us and the original texts had political agendas of their own, as well as a bevy of deeply held assumptions that they didn't even know they were assuming.

For example, scholars contend, with some justification, that the author who originally wrote down the seminal work from which the Tree of Life diagram is derived, the work we call *Sepher Yezirah* (though he might have been writing down an older oral tradition so it wouldn't be lost), was intent on contradicting Plato's assertion that the Supreme Being had need of a "plan"—a blueprint such as an architect would use. Other scholars dispute this point.

I, personally, don't care. The important point for me is that the assumptions and agendas of the transmitters of this wisdom aren't my assumptions and agendas. And the really vital point for me is that the Bible and the Tarot and the Tree of Life concept, and all the wisdom stored in them have no agenda or assumptions built into them that I can't understand and agree with. Furthermore, the ones that are built-in to the Tarot don't really resemble the ones the transmitting authors are "selling." In other words, through the ages, those who transmitted this wisdom and kept it alive for us to receive colored their understanding of it with the cultural assumptions and agendas of their day. Undoubtedly, I have done the same. So will you.

So, the Biblical text that relates to the Ace of Wands—and all Aces—is the very opening paragraph of the Bible. The translation I'm using is *The Torah, the Five Books of Moses, A New Translation of The Holy Scriptures* according to the Masoretic text, published in 1962 by The Jewish Publication Society of America, Philadelphia:

> *When God began to create the heaven and the earth—the earth being unformed and void, with darkness over the surface of the deep and a wind from God sweeping over the water—God said, "Let there be light"; and there was light.*

And that's the Ace of Wands—the very instant that simple "light" was allowed to "be".

Within human consciousness, the Ace of Wands represents the sensation you experience, the prickles over your skin, the sudden altering of your visual perception when the lighting seems brighter or dimmer, when sounds suddenly seem louder or recede into the distance, when you are engulfed by the feeling of falling over a cliff or ramming hard into a stone wall—all of that is the Ace of Wands manifesting in your body.

It can be either pleasant or unpleasant depending on your opinion of the content of the idea that has occurred to you. The characteristics that make this an Ace of Wands experience is that it is the first time a particular idea occurs to you. And what's more, this idea comes from outside the realities of your world—it challenges truths you hold self-evident.

The Ace of Wands is the single most abstract card in the Tarot deck, and the hardest to understand. And yet it is the single most common experience among human beings.

And that is the reason to learn Tarot. Not to foretell the future (which is impossible anyway and of no interest even if it were possible), but to acquire a language in which to think about thinking. If your language can't encompass it, you can't know it, you can't think it, and you can't think about it.

The Ace of Wands, like every other Tarot card, is a "word" in a language. Chances are you already know that language as a "jargon" that seems like English. It's the language of music, stories, poetry, graphic arts, color harmony, decorating, sculpture, choreography, and every other Art you can name, most especially the performing arts.

Learning to read Tarot is the process of figuring out which of the inner experiences that you are familiar with inside yourself are meant by this particular Tarot card.

Your personal experiences are unique to you. A Tarot card is general for everyone. By understanding which Tarot card pertains to your personal unique experience of life, how your individual experience of life connects to the general experience of archetypal humanity, you can learn to communicate your personal experience of life to other people whose experience is different from yours yet connected via that Archetype. And they never have to know that you are using a knowledge of Tarot to accomplish this. Furthermore, when someone tells you what they're feeling, your knowledge of Tarot can help you relate to their feelings.

It is as if something deep inside has said, "Let there be Light!" Ideas don't happen to you, as if you were a passive victim of some external Source that can bestow or withhold them at whim. Ideas are always there "without form and void, with darkness over the surface of the deep."

The parts of the Ace of Wands are the "Ace" or number One and the "Wand" or whatever the Wand symbolizes. The Ace of Wands is the first of The Minor Arcana, and the most abstract and difficult to comprehend. To make it more accessible I think of it this way: the essence of the meaning of One is "Being"—and the essence of the meaning of Wands is Idea. So Ace of Wands is "Idea is"—or "Idea into Being—or the beginning of an Idea." But there are other possibilities, some of which might suit you better.

This four-volume sub-set of *The Biblical Tarot* is subtitled "The Not So Minor Arcana" because there is nothing minor about the Minor Arcana. Each Minor Arcanum consists of a Number and a Suit—two independent variables. The "meaning" lies at the intersection or synthesis point of those two variables. That's only the beginning of the complexities.

So to begin to discover the meaning of a Tarot Card, you must first explore the nature of each independent variable, Suit and Number, and then try to bend your mind around what happens when you mix these two concepts. Then you look around inside yourself for something that corresponds to that mixture. Once you have that pegged, you search your external environment for something that corresponds to your internal referent.

That's how Eden Grey got all those nicely pre-cooked "meanings" to the cards. But if you look closely at the process I've outlined, you see all the times during that process where personal bias comes into the picture—personal opinion, personal prejudice. Do you really want to internalize someone else's personal prejudices? Don't you have enough trouble just dealing with your own?

So first let's explore the variable "Suit." Wands is a suit, like the playing card suit of Clubs. It's a sub-set of the deck, nothing more. Most instruction books will give you a deep mystical reason why the Wand is chosen as the symbol for this suit. Because there is so much glib mysticism around this symbol, artists have chosen to create decks using different symbols so they can claim different mystical meanings. But consider what the picture on the card actually does as far as reading Tarot is concerned.

You shuffle the cards, you cut them, you turn over a card and place it in front of you. You see, "It's the Ace of Wands." Your mind then associates, "Oh, Ace means beginning. Wands means ideas. This reading is about the beginning of an idea."

The picture of the Wand has triggered an association. It doesn't matter at all what the picture is as long as the association it triggers is correct.

There is one other aspect to associations that is important in Tarot reading: the association pathway that is most important in Tarot reading is the subconscious one. The symbols that work best are symbols that lead both the subconscious and the conscious mind onto the same associative pathway, so the two levels of your mind are singing two-part harmony. Thus the nature of the symbol that's best for you is partly dictated by your culture's symbols, partly by your personal emotional history, partly by your religion, partly by what you consciously think, believe, and would prefer to believe if only you could manage it, and partly by what you pretend you are when you know everyone is looking at you.

How your mind uses symbols to initiate association trains is a very idiosyncratic thing. In essence, it doesn't matter what symbols are drawn on the cards to distinguish the suits, as long as whatever you use for Wands represents for you the level of reality we're going to try to define next.

It doesn't matter what symbol you draw on your cards, it only matters that the symbol is associated for you with the top of the four Tree of Life diagrams. That's what gives this suit and its individual cards all their meanings—not the picture on the card, the underlying position of each card on this diagram which represents the structure of the universe as it was Created-out-of-Nothing.

That's why the Tarot works—because it is structured just like the universe is structured. Because it has the same structure, it resonates on the same frequencies as The Universe (i.e. The Music of the Spheres). Thus the Tarot helps you to see through the fog of life to the underlying skeleton that holds the universe together. Creation out of Nothing.

Another reason why this series of books is called *The Biblical Tarot* is because my entire approach to Tarot is via this underlying structure. This structure is called Jacob's Ladder, which has its origin in the Bible and the oral tradition that explains the Bible. And the Bible flatly, unequivocally, and categorically forbids fortune telling, in the sense of one person attempting to tell another person what will or won't happen to them in the future. And most especially not to pretend to predict the future for money or in the worship of some other god (which is what the fortune tellers "sitting in the gates of the city" did—they read entrails and clouds and knucklebones in the worship of various gods who would arrange a nice future for you for a mere pittance of a bribe).

The Suit of Wands then represents the topmost of the Tree of Life diagram—but what does that topmost Tree represent? Actually there are four Tree of Life diagrams called the Four Worlds of the Qabalah. I don't like the term "worlds" because it's very misleading in English. It's a level of reality. But what does that mean?

Books will tell you the Four Worlds correspond to the Four Alchemical elements: Earth, Air, Fire, and Water. But of course the Alchemical elements have nothing to do with chemistry. They have to do with subjective mental states of awareness, psychological and philosophical ways of being and the transformation of one way into another.

The scholars get involved again and start arguing about whether Wands corresponds to Fire or Swords corresponds to Fire. Dion Fortune uses Wands to correspond to Fire, and that's as good a convention as we need, so let's use it. It's just a convention. It doesn't really matter. What matters is that however which way you start—keep using that symbolism, so your subconscious doesn't get confused. Repetition and consistency is what's important here—not the shape of the doodle drawn on the card.

So, okay, Wands equals Fire, but what's "Fire"? It's not the kind you keep in your fireplace. What we're really talking about with the concept "Fire" is the level of creation that Qabalah terms Atziluth.

It is the closest of the four levels to where God is. Thus it is the most abstract, the most archetypal, the merest outline of reality (a sketch), the surveyor's string going from wooden stake to wooden stake outlining the foundation of where the building will be. Keep in mind here that the anonymous author of *Sepher Yezirah* went to great pains to avoid the concept of "blueprint." To create-something-from-nothing the Creator didn't need a blueprint. But to create something-from-something, mortals do need a blueprint. And so from the diagramless *Sepher Yezirah* we derive the glyph we call Jacob's Ladder—our blueprint!

"Wands" is only an indication, a suggestion, a hint of what might yet be. It's a plan, a hope, a dream, a wish. Do you see? "Wands" represents IDEA—but idea is only one way to say what it represents. It represents a whole lot more than Idea.

There is no one English word that can say "Wands" that can mean *Atziluth*. It is a concept that modern American English vernacular doesn't deal with on a daily basis, so there is no word for it. Beginning? Downbeat? The word "And!" when spoken in that unique declarative used by ballet instructors to signal the moment *before* movement must begin. That is the level of *Atziluth*. The prelude. The indrawn breath of the singer *before* that singular pure note. The moment of awareness *before* you awaken in the morning—the moment when it is most effective to pray.

The other component of the Ace of Wands is the Ace

part, called Ace because in the playing deck Ace means One and in many games the Ace has some special rules that don't apply to other cards. It is "singular" or "unique." But One is just as good a name to call it. The One of Wands is the single highest point on the Ladder, the closest to the Ineffable. It is the singular POINT at which creation begins. It is unformed, unstructured, powerfully bright with excess energy bursting to spill over into the next one down, the Two. This POINT has no dimension (which is the definition of POINT after all). It's not long, not high, not wide, not deep. It is a single POINT, a hole in the fabric of creation through which energy spills from OUTSIDE and collects until it spills over into Two.

In Qabalah, whole huge encyclopedic works have been written about the concept One. But it all boils down to one simple fact which you can study your whole life and not begin to grasp—that God is One. That's it. That's the whole thing. You don't need to know anything else if you know that, least of all Tarot. Of course knowing that isn't something anyone is likely to achieve in a mere mortal lifespan. Fortunately, we aren't commanded to complete the Work, only not to desist from it.

Another word used to designate the circles on the Tree of Life is "Vessels." They Receive what is emanated through that dimensionless point at the top of the uppermost Tree. Understand yourself as the 'vessel" and, if you can make yourself "have an idea" slowly enough that you can watch it happen, you can feel something pouring into you—just in that moment before the "Aha! I've got it!!"

So "One" is really a "place" or perhaps a "state," a condition of being whole, indivisible, or at least undivided. The single germ cell before it first divides—but it contains the "code" for the entire new organism that will grow from it and all its progeny to follow. It's where you go to get anything started. It's deep inside yourself where you are One with God. And God will only come within you by invitation—remember that!

You're not a victim at the whim of some external power. You don't sit around waiting for inspiration to strike. You go "there" and you move your breath upon your waters. And you invite. And there is Light. And that process is the Ace of Wands. But you need a blueprint because you can only create something-out-of-something. Still, that creation is also Divine—and it is the most profound kind of worship I know how to do.

Therefore, the Ace of Wands is a group of bored seven-year-old children on a stormy day, strewn around the living room in inert disarray just before the moment when one of them lunges upright and cries, "I know! I've got an idea what we can do!" And all the children take fire. Two hours later, the house is a shambles—but in that preternatural peace before the initiating cry there was One, and then there was Wand, and *boom* the Big Bang—

Watch for volume 2 in the Biblical Tarot series "The Magic of the Wands"

Index

Belfry Books Order Form. Order direct from publisher
Please ship the enclosed Belfry Books order to:

Name_____

Address_____

City_____ State_____ Zip_____

P L E A S E   P R I N T   C L E A R L Y

All payments in U.S. funds only. Check, Money Order or International M.O.
Canadian prices slightly higher. Contact publisher for pricing.

Title	Price Ea.	Qnty.	Amount
Now Available			
The Amityville Horror Conspiracy	14.95		
Teachings of the Winged Disk	14.95		
Upcoming Titles			
Dancing With Devas	14.95		
Haunted Pennsylvania	14.95		
Deadly Town	14.95		
	Subtotal		
Shipping & Handling 1.55 per book			
	Total enclosed		

Mail completed order form to:
Toad Hall, Inc.
Rural Route 2 Box 16-B
Laceyville, PA 18623

Belfry Books

Hannah M.G. Shapero

Illustration and fine art

Featured on the cover
and interior illustrations
of this book

Hannah M.G.Shapero
2224 Pimmit Run Lane #203
Falls Church, Virginia 22043
hmgs@access.digex.net
http://www.walker.reston.va.us/hmgs

Full service print media, from
vague idea to "camera ready" art
for film output.

- **Small Press & Periodicals**
- **B&W & Process Color**
- **Art Direction**
- **Electronic Layout**
- **PageMaker & Photoshop**
- **Scanning**
- **Optical & Zip Disk**

Steven Dale
805 254-3319
FAX 805 288-1754
dale1der@ecom.net

23420 Happy Valley Drive
Newhall, CA 91321

Never Cross A Palm With Silver
Production cover design and
interior pages by Steven Dale
Produced on a Macintosh™
Quadra 630
All images were manipulated in
ADOBE Photoshop™
Page layouts were done in
ADOBE Pagemaker™
Periperials are UMAX™ scanner,
DELTIS Olympus MO drive and a
Iomega ZIP™ drive
Color monitor is a 15" SAMSUNG
SyncMaster 4Ne